50K LIONS OF JUSTICE

SEPTEMBER 23, 2018

STAND UP FOR HOPE AND RESPECT

DAISAKU IKEDA

STAND UP FOR HOPE AND RESPECT!

ESSENTIALS OF THE SOKA GAKKAI SPIRIT

DAISAKU IKEDA

World Tribune Press

Published by WORLD TRIBUNE PRESS
A division of the SGI-USA
606 Wilshire Blvd.
Santa Monica, CA 90401

Printed in the United States of America.

Cover and interior design by *the*BookDesigners

CONTENTS

EDITOR'S NOTE

Stand Up for Hope and Respect: Essentials of the Soka Gakkai Spirit is a collection of brief comments by SGI President Ikeda from his series titled "Humanistic Teachings for Victory." Through the series, the SGI president sought to convey the Soka Gakkai spirit to youth members by touching on various aspects of faith and practice and drawing on his own experiences in life and faith.

The citations most commonly used in this book have been abbreviated as follows:

LSOC, page number(s) refers to *The Lotus Sutra and Its Opening and Closing Sutras,* translated by Burton Watson (Tokyo: Soka Gakkai, 2009).

OTT, page number(s) refers to *The Record of the Orally Transmitted Teachings,* translated by Burton Watson (Tokyo: Soka Gakkai, 2004).

WND, page number(s) refers to *The Writings of Nichiren Daishonin,* vol. 1 (WND-1) (Tokyo: Soka Gakkai, 1999) and vol. 2 (WND-2) (Tokyo: Soka Gakkai, 2006).

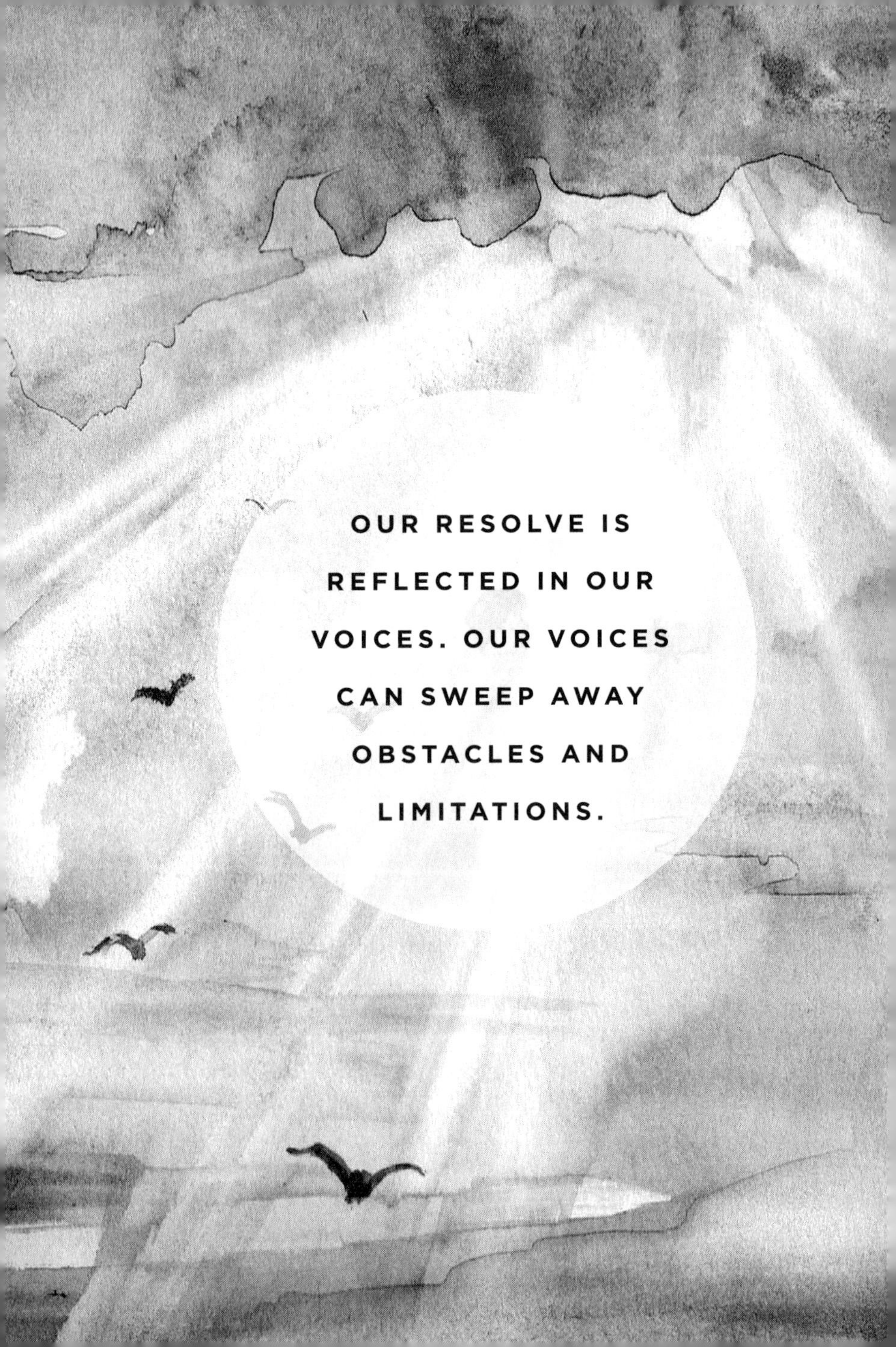

OUR RESOLVE IS REFLECTED IN OUR VOICES. OUR VOICES CAN SWEEP AWAY OBSTACLES AND LIMITATIONS.

1

THE VOICE DOES THE BUDDHA'S WORK

Chanting Nam-myoho-renge-kyo is the foundation of our Buddhist practice. Let's always make a point of chanting vibrantly with the invigorating rhythm of a magnificent steed galloping freely across wide open plains.

Chanting Nam-myoho-renge-kyo inspires us to action and gives us strength and energy. It is the source of forward momentum.

Even a single utterance of Nam-myoho-renge-kyo reverberates throughout the universe. The sound of the Mystic Law cannot fail to awaken and activate the protective forces of the universe.

• • •

Once when I led a group of members in chanting Nam-myoho-renge-kyo three times, their voices weren't in unison. It also meant that they weren't united in spirit as they prepared to undertake a new challenge. If they lacked unity, they wouldn't be able to display their full potential nor achieve tangible results. I chanted three times with them again and again until they could do it in unison.

Then I had them join together in proclaiming "Forward!" At first, their voices were weak, but with each successive try they steadily grew in strength and vigor. Eventually all the members brimmed with the determination and confidence to advance.

Our resolve is reflected in our voices. Our voices can sweep away obstacles and limitations. When the members that day were finally able to speak with strong and confident voices, their dynamic advance to victory began.

* * *

The success of meetings is also determined by our voices. I hope you will hold meetings that resound with vibrant, confident voices.

I particularly ask the event staff and behind-the-scenes group members to do their utmost to give everyone a warm welcome and send-off, showing them the courtesy and respect befitting a Buddha. Your cheerful greetings are sure to brighten the hearts of the participants, who have taken the time out of their busy schedules to attend.

If you see someone who seems to be feeling poorly, ask them if they need any help. Remind everyone on the way out to take care and get home safely. Such considerate words protect life. A voice infused with a powerful wish and determination to keep the members from harm will dispel devilish functions.

The voice does the Buddha's work. Let's use our voices to do just that!

2

CONFIDENTLY TALKING TO OTHERS ABOUT BUDDHISM

Sharing Buddhism requires courage. Please confidently talk to others about the greatness of Nichiren Buddhism and the benefit of our Buddhist practice.

Nichiren Daishonin writes, "Because one has heard the Lotus Sutra, which leads to Buddhahood, with this as the seed, one will invariably become a Buddha" (WND-1, 882).

Just speak freely and openly about your own convictions and experiences in faith. Whether the other person listens or not, you will have planted the seed of happiness and hope. That seed will someday definitely sprout, send down roots, and bring forth shoots that will eventually flower.

• • •

Introducing someone to the practice of Nichiren Buddhism can be extremely challenging. The Lotus Sutra states that the Mystic Law is "difficult to believe and difficult to understand" (LSOC, 173). That's why nothing is more noble or commendable than efforts to share Buddhism with others.

In my youth, I also had a very hard time introducing others to Buddhism, but I persevered steadfastly together with my fellow members. We encouraged and assured one another that though no one might decide to practice today, millions were waiting for our message.

Always be positive and upbeat when you share Nichiren Buddhism, whether others decide to practice or not. The aim of our dialogue, after all, is to impart great hope and courage to others.

To ponder and worry about how you can help others become happy is in itself a truly noble thing, isn't it? Such concern for others is the concern of Bodhisattvas of the Earth and the concern of the Buddha.

Helping someone enshrine the Gohonzon is an event as wonderful as bringing Nichiren to their home.

• • •

The second Soka Gakkai president, Josei Toda, often said with regard to propagation: "There is no special technique for introducing others to Buddhism. The key is simply to chant earnestly to the Gohonzon."

Sharing Buddhism with others starts from your prayers for the other person's happiness. They will definitely feel the sincerity of your intent. It is your heart that touches and moves others' hearts.

When you sincerely speak the truth, you can build trust. Trust is youth's greatest treasure.

The more you share Nichiren Buddhism with others, the more the Buddha nature inherent in your own life and theirs will be strengthened and the more the indestructible treasures of the heart will accumulate in the depths of both your life and theirs.

3

THE STRATEGY OF THE LOTUS SUTRA—WINNING BASED ON CHANTING

It is important that we put chanting Nam-myoho-renge-kyo first. We must start by earnestly chanting. Why do we chant? To strengthen our lives and bring out our potential to the fullest extent.

Nichiren Daishonin writes: "The mighty sword of the Lotus Sutra [Nam-myoho-renge-kyo] must be wielded by one courageous in faith. Then one will be as strong as a demon armed with an iron staff" (WND-1, 412).

We need to break through the limitations of our lesser self and devote ourselves wholeheartedly to spreading the Mystic Law—discarding the negligent tendency to cut corners and do the least amount of work possible and the arrogance to think that our own shallow strategies will somehow carry us through. Nothing is more powerful than chanting Nam-myoho-renge-kyo based on the vow to win for the sake of kosen-rufu.

Youth who chant never regress. When we chant, we embark on a path to victory. Those who take action based on prayer win in the end.

* * *

Regarding prayer based on the Mystic Law, Nichiren Daishonin writes that there is "conspicuous prayer and conspicuous response, conspicuous prayer and inconspicuous response, inconspicuous prayer and inconspicuous response, and inconspicuous prayer and conspicuous response" (WND-1, 750). Sometimes our prayers may be answered immediately, while at other times we can see no clear response. But whatever the case, the important thing is that we keep chanting Nam-myoho-renge-kyo with unwavering faith in the Gohonzon. We need to keep chanting earnestly and keep chanting right through to the very end.

Even if it seems our prayers haven't been answered, everything will ultimately move in the best possible direction for our lives. We will be able to build lives of incredible joy that makes all our struggles worthwhile. Such is the great power of the Mystic Law.

* * *

An arrow will not hit the target unless we take proper aim. The same is true of chanting. Our prayers come to fruition when we set clear goals and strive earnestly and persistently to realize them.

Faith in the realm of Nichiren Buddhism is not a matter of simply chanting to the Gohonzon and expecting things to automatically go well. We need to chant and make efforts, make efforts and chant; by doing so, we can activate the positive functions of the universe to work on our behalf.

Paraphrasing Nichiren, Mr. Toda said, "If you can't cross a moat ten feet wide, how can you possibly hope to cross a moat twenty or thirty feet wide? (see WND-1, 808). You have to work steadily and patiently at accomplishing each goal you have set."

When we lose sight of our goals, we start going around in circles and getting nowhere.

Chant specifically about your goals for the coming day, and then do your best to act on those goals, striving wholeheartedly in a way that befits youth.

4

NICHIREN'S WRITINGS ARE THE ETERNAL FOUNDATION OF THE SGI

"Exert yourself in the two ways of practice and study" (WND-1, 386), writes Nichiren Daishonin. The important thing is that you continue to study Nichiren's writings and put what you have learned into practice. Even if you can't remember everything you've studied, some of it will remain with you, engraved in the depths of your life. At a crucial moment, it will enable you to bring forth the power of faith to overcome the challenge before you.

Those who have a solid body of teachings as their guide are strong. The source for all victory is found in the collected writings of Nichiren Daishonin. That's why I'd like you, the youth, to thoroughly study them while you are still young. It will form a foundation for happiness for the rest of your lives and give you the strength to always emerge victorious.

• • •

It's important to read Nichiren's writings each day—even if just a sentence or a paragraph—making it part of your daily life and activities for kosen-rufu. Do your best to study and understand the Daishonin's message. If you apply yourself earnestly, you'll be able to absorb the meaning of his words into your life, as if by osmosis.

My mentor, Mr. Toda, said, "You should read each line of Nichiren's writings with a deep personal conviction in its truth." There is a difference between understanding something intellectually and understanding it on the level of faith.

If you apply the Daishonin's words to your own life, the time is certain to come when you can say, "Ah, that's what he's talking about!" and you will fully grasp his meaning.

• • •

When we lecture on Nichiren's writings, we should do so sincerely and confidently as representatives of our mentor. I always gave such lectures with the spirit that I was representing Mr. Toda.

Nichiren's writings brim with the fearless courage of the lion king and the irrepressible compassion of the Buddha to help all people attain enlightenment. The Daishonin is personally encouraging us. His writings are filled with encouragement—encouragement to which our lives cannot fail to respond.

I hope you'll readily share with others how the Daishonin's teachings have touched your life and given you courage. It doesn't matter if you're an eloquent speaker or not; what matters is your firm resolve to encourage others based on the Daishonin's words.

Why has the SGI grown to the extent it has today? Because we have striven to wholeheartedly encourage others based on a profound philosophy of life. Let us all continue to study Nichiren's writings and share what we have learned with others.

5

THE NOBLE OBJECTIVE OF ADVANCING KOSEN-RUFU

What is the SGI's fundamental aim? It is to realize peace and happiness for all humanity. It is to enable everyone to attain an inner state of being in which life itself is a joy and delight. This is kosen-rufu; this is our noble objective.

My mentor, Josei Toda, said that it was his wish to rid the world of misery.

Those who strive for the incomparably great goal of kosen-rufu become great individuals themselves. A towering objective is a towering source of inspiration.

Let's dedicate ourselves joyfully and energetically to actualizing the great vow for kosen-rufu. Let's strive our hardest—in our jobs and our communities and in our SGI activities—for the sake of kosen-rufu, for our friends, and for ourselves.

• • •

I hope that all of you will chant and challenge yourselves earnestly to see how far forward you can take our movement for kosen-rufu during your generation.

Mr. Toda once said, "We of the Soka Gakkai—committed to protecting life, the most precious treasure in all the world—count how many people we have introduced to the Mystic Law and led to happiness."

In the SGI, numbers aren't just statistics—they represent precious individual lives. They encapsulate people's happiness.

That's why it's important for us to set goals, value each individual, and help one person after another form a connection with Nichiren Buddhism.

Our great network for peace and happiness expands and grows by gaining the understanding of one person at a time.

• • •

Buddhism is about winning. So is life. That's why it's important for you to exert yourselves and win.

Aim to be the best in something. If you content yourself with achieving second or third best from the outset, you won't be able to tap your full potential.

The spirit to keep making efforts with the resolve "I vow to be the best, even if I still have a long way to go!" will bring you immeasurable benefit and a lofty life.

Create an enduring personal record of striving your hardest to be the best. Those who do so are true victors.

6

UNITY IS A POWERFUL FORCE FOR VICTORY

Unity is strength. We must unite in order to win.

How can we achieve unity? First, leaders themselves have to stand up as individuals. It's not up to others; we ourselves have to stand up resolutely.

Mr. Toda declared: "Youth, just one of you stand! A second and then a third will definitely follow!" This is the formula for victory.

Merely calling out for unity doesn't unite people's hearts. Leaders need to earnestly chant and wholeheartedly praise their fellow members. Joyful unity for victory will be achieved when you respect your fellow members and appreciate your good fortune in being able to work together with them for kosen-rufu.

• • •

Unity does not mean forcing everyone into a single, uniform mold. Nichiren Daishonin writes, "If the spirit of many in body but one in mind prevails among the people, they will achieve all their goals, whereas if one in body but different in mind, they can achieve nothing remarkable" (WND-1, 618).

He says "many in body," not "one in body." It is important for us to respect one another's individuality, assist and support one another in a spirit of friendship and goodwill, and enable all to make the most of their unique qualities.

"Mind" of "one in mind" refers to "faith." Mr. Toda said, "If you, the youth, develop a strong commitment in faith—the stronger, the better—you will never be defeated by any difficulty you encounter." Let our youthful SGI always advance with the spirit of "many in body, one in mind."

We must start by chanting with unity of purpose or shared commitment. In all my efforts, I chanted with the powerful resolve to win for the sake of kosen-rufu and my mentor. I also chanted for my fellow members who were striving valiantly alongside me. And even in leading the members in chanting Nam-myoho-renge-kyo three times, I earnestly strove to get everyone to chant together in solid unity for our goal.

When people work together in this way, their combined power grows not by the simple arithmetic of 1 + 1 = 2, but exponentially to become ten or one hundred. This positive, multiplication effect is the wonder of unity in faith. Teamwork based on mutual trust and support is a source of tremendous momentum.

Our organization is truly a gathering of diverse individuals. All of them have a noble mission; all of them are Buddhas worthy of respect. Instead of judging people based on your own assumptions, chant to the Gohonzon and embrace everyone with a big heart as you work together to advance kosen-rufu.

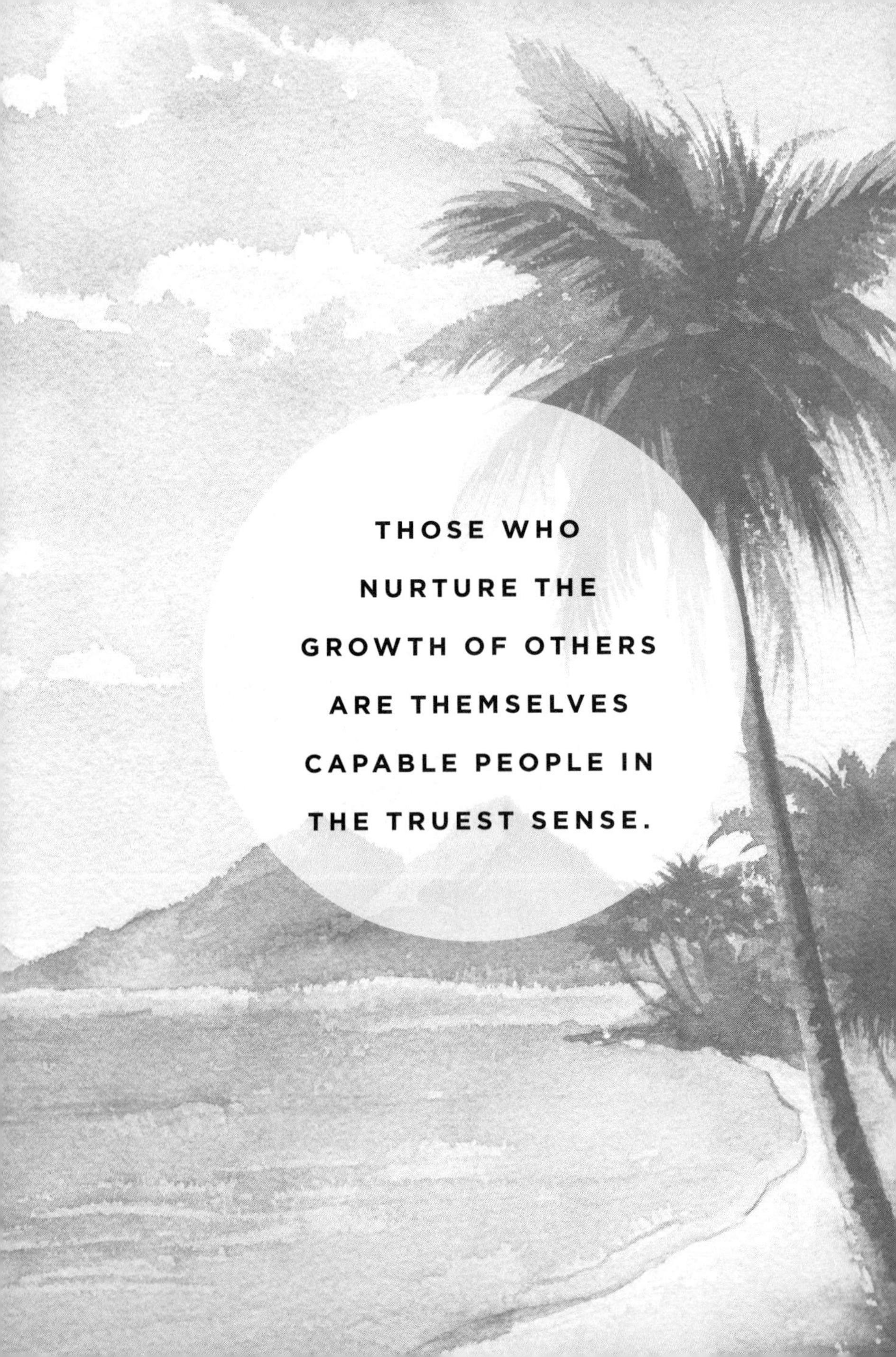

THOSE WHO
NURTURE THE
GROWTH OF OTHERS
ARE THEMSELVES
CAPABLE PEOPLE IN
THE TRUEST SENSE.

7

THE KEY TO SUCCESS IS FOSTERING CAPABLE PEOPLE

"We must make the Soka Gakkai a bastion of capable people!" So declared President Toda.

Everything depends on people. The presence of individuals who can advance kosen-rufu will pave the way to greater victory for our movement.

Don't complain that there aren't any capable members in your area. Instead, start by becoming a truly capable person for kosen-rufu yourself. When one person stands up, another and then another will follow. This is the principle of "emerging from the earth" (WND-1, 385). If you chant with the firm conviction that there are definitely other people in your area who can play an active role for kosen-rufu—and if you keep working on your own personal growth—you'll discover them.

Let's find capable people, meet and talk with them, sincerely chant for their growth, and then strive to foster them one after another. Those who nurture the growth of others are themselves capable people in the truest sense.

• • •

Value your fellow members, especially your juniors. I always treasured our youth in accord with the Daishonin's teaching "Become as inseparable as fish and the water in which they swim" (WND-1, 217). I was overjoyed to be able to witness their growth, because I knew they would all be shouldering the SGI into the future.

Praise your juniors' strong points and encourage them to develop them. And when you have to draw their attention to a problem, do so in a way that makes your point effectively. Don't arrogantly scold them. Sincere encouragement is the best teaching method.

Fostering juniors with the prayer and sense of responsibility that they go on to surpass us in ability is an SGI tradition.

An earnest wish for someone to become a capable successor for kosen-rufu will definitely be realized.

• • •

Together is the byword for fostering capable people. Chant together, study together, talk together, do activities together, and sometimes have coffee or a meal together—it's important to advance together enjoyably in this way.

Nichiren Daishonin says, "'Joy' means that oneself and others together experience joy" (OTT, 146). When we rejoice at and praise one another's growth, we will savor unsurpassed joy and fulfillment.

The spirit to foster our juniors also promotes unity. As fellow members, let's all take a step forward together for victory!

8

DISCUSSION MEETINGS—THE DRIVING FORCE FOR KOSEN-RUFU

Discussion meetings are the lifeline for the progress of the SGI.

It was also thanks to a discussion meeting that I was able to encounter my mentor, Josei Toda.

The driving force for the development of kosen-rufu is first and foremost small gatherings where people can meet face to face; it is heart-to-heart discussion. The SGI has won over all obstacles because we have forged strong personal bonds with our fellow members.

Mr. Toda placed great importance on discussion meetings. Even when there were only a few participants, he was delighted and did his best to make the meeting a success, knowing that smaller gatherings allowed for deeper discussion.

Nothing is more powerful than steady, grass-roots activities.

The ongoing effort of challenging ourselves from one discussion meeting to the next is the rhythm of victory that has become the tradition of the SGI.

• • •

Mr. Toda declared that kosen-rufu will be realized through discussion meetings.

The presence of a single youth can transform the discussion meeting. The arrival of a single youth can instantly brighten the atmosphere. Above all, there is nothing more uplifting than attending lively discussion meetings in which youth play an active role.

From my days in the youth division, I would always prepare to make each discussion meeting enjoyable and satisfying by chanting for the happiness of each guest and each of my fellow members.

The efforts of the youth can revolutionize discussion meetings and give fresh momentum to the development of our movement.

• • •

Discussion meetings brim with the Buddhist philosophy for leading a winning life. They provide us with inspiration as we learn from the lives of others. They are schools of humanism firmly grounded in the people. I hope you will eagerly seek to learn from such gatherings. Nichiren Daishonin also encourages those with a strong seeking spirit in faith to gather together in one place and listen to the teachings of Buddhism (see WND-1, 206).

Sharing our experiences and studying Buddhism together—this is the most correct path of Buddhist practice. Let's talk and share freely at discussion meetings.

Nothing is more powerful than the voices of youth. When youth speak, they can invigorate both themselves and those present at the meeting. Through the power of youth, please make each meeting a gathering that imparts hope, courage, and vigor to all.

9

PRAYING FOR THE HAPPINESS OF ALL SGI YOUNG WOMEN

With the same spirit as my mentor, it is my prayer and wish for all our young women's division members to become happy.

Nichiren Daishonin writes, "Those who now believe in the Lotus Sutra will gather fortune from ten thousand miles away" (WND-1, 1137). Since you embrace faith in the Mystic Law from your youth, there is no doubt that you will attain happiness.

Reality can be harsh, and life is long. That is why faith and a sound life philosophy are so important.

By possessing from the time of your youth the unerring spiritual compass of Buddhist study, you can walk the correct path in life, become truly happy without fail, and achieve wonderful victories.

• • •

Seek out friends you can trust, rely on, and consult with, and resolve to become such an individual yourself.

Mr. Toda said, "Make friends with even just one person whom you can share your heart with or who can teach you about faith in times of need."

Youth is a time of grappling with problems. But it is only because you have such struggles that you can grow and become an outstanding individual.

Since you possess within you the supreme treasure of the Mystic Law, you have nothing to fear. Even if your efforts go unnoticed by others, the Gohonzon is aware of everything, and all the Buddhas and heavenly deities throughout the universe will definitely protect you. So please don't worry about anything. Have confidence in yourself, and just do your very best.

• • •

The young women's division holds the key to the future of the SGI. One capable young woman can exhibit the power of ten or even a hundred people. If the young women's division continues to develop joyfully, the SGI will also continue to flourish and triumph.

Expand your network of friendship among young women! People will gather where there is a lively, bright, and enjoyable atmosphere.

May each of you shine in your own way with the Kayo-kai* spirit and create a brilliant record of achievement that gives you a proud sense of accomplishment and valuable experiences in faith.

* "Kayo-kai" literally means "Flower-Sun Group."

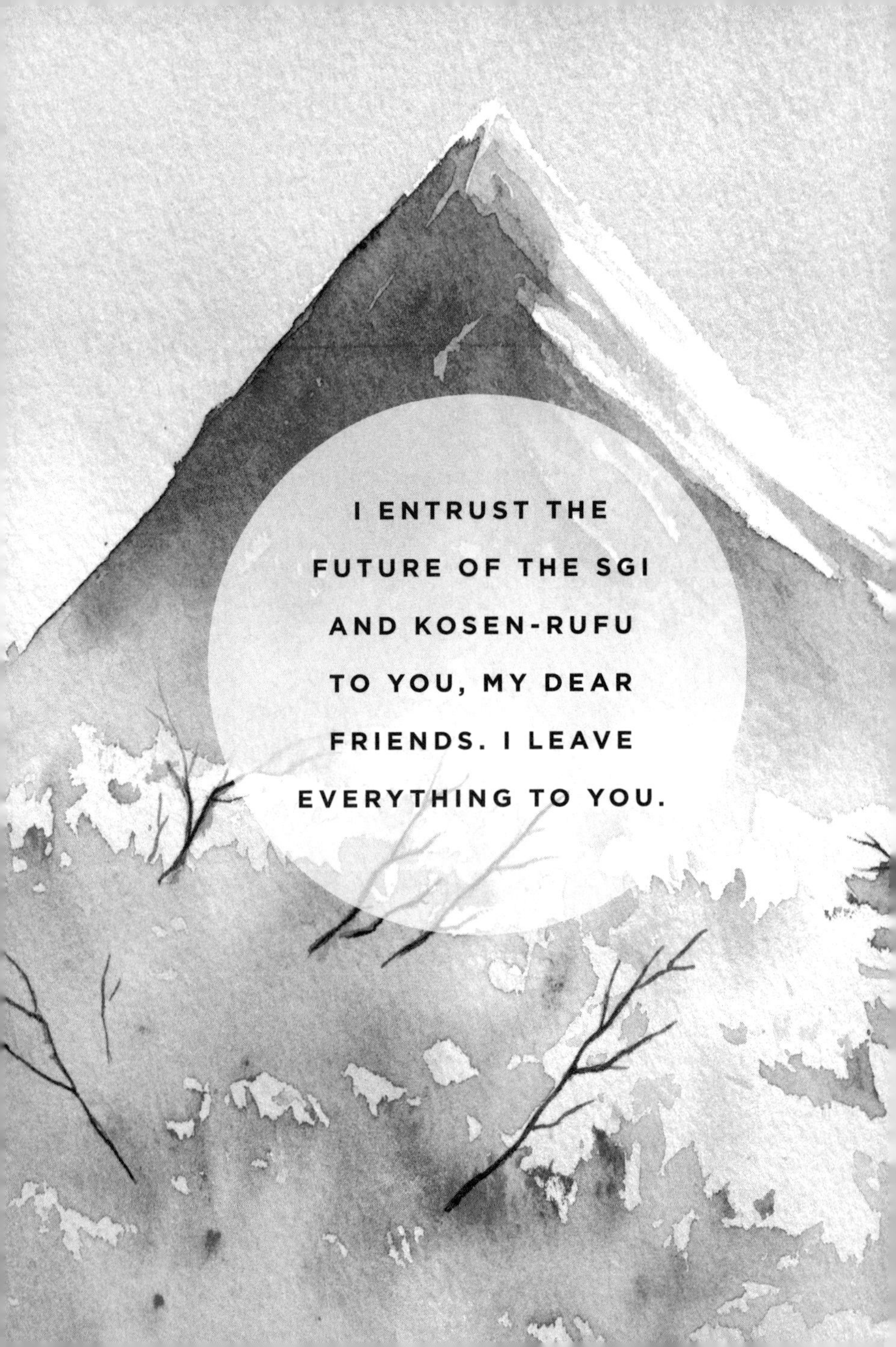

I ENTRUST THE FUTURE OF THE SGI AND KOSEN-RUFU TO YOU, MY DEAR FRIENDS. I LEAVE EVERYTHING TO YOU.

10

STUDENTS, LEAD A VIBRANT YOUTH OF MISSION!

As mentor and disciple, Mr. Toda and I built the student division. Mr. Toda was delighted when the division was formed. Having taken on the problems of ordinary people as his own and fought head-on against the devilish nature of authority, he eagerly awaited the emergence of genuine leaders who combined both courage and intellect.

Nichiren Daishonin states that the widespread propagation of the Mystic Law throughout the world is actualized "due to the authority and supernatural power of Bodhisattva Universal Worthy" (OTT, 190). Kosen-rufu will be achieved when universally worthy and wise youth take their place at the forefront of our movement and expand our ranks of capable individuals.

You can't defend the welfare of the people if you don't know the first thing about hard work. Therefore, through your struggles to fulfill your noble mission, please develop your intellect and character and grow into leaders who will usher in a new age.

• • •

The purpose of learning is to contribute to people's happiness, to serve humanity, to repay one's debt of gratitude to one's parents, and to create a bright, successful future. Those who keep learning are never defeated.

I never stopped learning, even in the midst of my earnest struggles to support and assist my mentor. The many conversations I have conducted with world leaders, bridging cultures and civilizations, are a victorious testimony of my assiduous studies at "Toda University."*

The Mystic Law is the wellspring of wisdom that enables us to make the best use of everything in our lives. All of you, while still young, are advancing along the admirable path of putting faith into action through your studies and applying Buddhism in society. I hope you will spend your youth meaningfully in the pursuit of learning and self-cultivation.

• • •

Passion like the sun, wisdom like the moonlight, courage like a lion king, and solidarity like a bamboo grove—these are the hallmarks of the student division. You, my young friends of the student division, are sources of shining hope. You are opening the way to peace, justice, and human victory.

* "Toda University": Unable to attend university because of his work and other commitments, Daisaku Ikeda received private instruction from his mentor, Josei Toda, a renowned educator.

"We can trust the youth. The youth are our only hope"—this was Mr. Toda's belief. He encouraged the student division members, telling them that they had a greater mission than they imagined. And he was confident that they would all go on to become outstanding individuals.

Because I, too, believe in you, I say to you: Be bold! Be courageous! Be invincible!

I entrust the future of the SGI and kosen-rufu to you, my dear friends. I leave everything to you.

THE VOICE OF TRUTH IS THE SPARK THAT AWAKENS OTHERS. YOUNG PEOPLE HAVE A SPECIAL MISSION IN THIS REGARD.

11

THE SPIRIT OF "REFUTING THE ERRONEOUS AND REVEALING THE TRUE"

The principle of establishing the correct teaching for the peace of the land is the essence of Nichiren Buddhism. Nichiren Daishonin directly confronted the devilish nature in human life that inflicts suffering and misery on people.

Only by refuting error can the truth be established. It is crucial that the youth of the SGI blaze with the dauntless spirit of "refuting the erroneous and revealing the true," just like Nichiren Daishonin.

Truth is strength. We must courageously demonstrate that strength, letting it resonate as powerful conviction in our words.

My mentor Josei Toda, often said, "Advance with courage and confidence!"

Therefore, while always being gentle to those who are suffering, let's be resolute in our opposition to corruption and wrongdoing, with the same spirit as the Daishonin. When we take action for the sake of good in this way, we will gain benefit without fail.

• • •

We use our voices to refute the erroneous and reveal the true. When we speak in earnest, we can vanquish devilish functions. Our vibrant, invigorating voices can completely change others' hearts. The important thing is for us to share our convictions with honesty and courage. The voice of truth is the spark that awakens others. Young people have a special mission in this regard.

Nichiren Daishonin writes: "Each of you should summon up the courage of a lion king and never succumb to threats from anyone. The lion king fears no other beast, nor do its cubs. Slanderers are like barking foxes, but Nichiren's followers are like roaring lions" (WND-1, 997). He is calling on his disciples to speak out with the same spirit as he did. The united declarations of mentor and disciple are the roars of lions.

• • •

President Toda said to us youth: "If you would be my disciples, you mustn't allow yourselves to be defeated by any false or erroneous arguments. You need to demolish them and show them for the falsehoods they are!" It is the pride and honor of my youth that I unswervingly followed this course.

The Latter Day of the Law is an age of quarrels and disputes. It is a time when words are wildly distorted and truth and falsehood are turned on their heads. If the forces dedicated to good lose vitality and strength, the people will suffer and society will fall into disarray.

Young people need to acquire the ability to tell the difference between truth and falsehood. They need to respond vigorously to malicious slanders and defamations that are aimed at discrediting those who champion good and at undermining their unity. Youth mustn't be timid or fainthearted.

With youth in the lead, let's talk honestly and forge ties of trust with as many people as possible.

12

YOUTH, STAND UP WITH SELF-RELIANCE!

My mentor gave us the eternal guideline to make our organization a citadel built of capable people.

The citadel of the SGI is a place where capable people study and train themselves—where they grow and develop as human beings. It is a place where capable people foster other capable people, thereby expanding our movement for peace, culture, and education. It is also a place where capable people take the initiative to win in the struggle to fulfill the mission of realizing a peaceful society through spreading the humanistic principles and ideals of Nichiren Buddhism. Furthermore, it is a citadel that flourishes through the shared struggle and victory of mentor and disciple as they strive toward the same goal, with the same sense of responsibility and spirit.

All of our SGI training groups—including such behind-the-scenes support groups as the Soka Group, Gajokai, and Byakuren—are crucial mainstays of our great citadel of capable people dedicated to kosen-rufu. Those who have received training in the music corps, the fife and drum corps, and so forth, have also developed splendidly and are making wonderful contributions to kosen-rufu. Each one of these members is my direct disciple.

I hope that all of you, our youth division members, will proudly lead the way in every struggle with sincerity, dedication, and boldness.

• • •

When youth stand up with a self-reliant spirit, they truly shine. Please take action with a sense of personal responsibility for kosen-rufu rather than leaving it up to others. The SGI is a place for you to train yourself to do this. Now is the time for you to work really hard. The greater the efforts you make, the more you will be able to forge and polish your life. You will definitely be able to win in the end.

I also took on all challenges myself, pondering, agonizing, and praying deeply about how best to move forward. I had no time to complain. There is surely no more noble way to spend your youth than taking on organizational responsibilities for the sake of kosen-rufu. You can leave behind an eternal record of achievement.

• • •

Mr. Toda often remarked, "The Soka Gakkai organization is more precious than my own life." The pure heritage of faith in the Mystic Law flows in the SGI whose members strive in the beautiful unity of "many in body, one in mind." That's why we must always advance with the welfare of members as our top priority. This is all-important. Fellow members should respect and encourage one another as if they were Buddhas.

Let's treasure each person. Let's empower each person. From there, kosen-rufu will spread far and wide—herein lies the proud mission and honor of the SGI.

13

BECOME LEADERS OF DEEP CONVICTION

It is crucial for leaders to have deep conviction in the power of the Mystic Law. When we believe in the Gohonzon, no prayer will go unanswered (see WND-1, 345). As leaders, let's always start with earnestly chanting Nam-myoho-renge-kyo and striving our hardest. Let's win in all struggles for the sake of our fellow members and for kosen-rufu.

Nichiren writes, "This Gohonzon also is found only in the two characters for faith"* (WND-1, 832). Faith determines everything. Through bringing forth the great power of faith and practice, we can limitlessly tap the vast and immeasurable power of the Buddha and the Law embodied in the Gohonzon. As a result, we can defeat all devilish functions and resolutely protect many fellow members.

• • •

A leader is another name for one who strives with courage. A dynamic spiritual current flows through such individuals, making them shine. Their powerful commitment draws others to them like a magnet and inspires those people to stand

* The Japanese word for *faith* consists of two Chinese characters.

up and take action. They are able to unite people's hearts.

It's not about strategies or methods. When you strive in faith, earnestly determined to take full responsibility, boundless wisdom will well up from within you.

Being appointed a leader for kosen-rufu and working hard to actively support your fellow members will enable you to be a great leader throughout the three existences of past, present, and future. This is the Buddhist law of cause and effect.

• • •

The SGI is forever committed to offering sound guidance in faith. Offering guidance in faith is essentially encouraging members to chant to the Gohonzon.

When members come to you with their problems, listen sincerely and attentively. If you don't know how to advise them, take them to see someone who can. This is also an important part of offering guidance.

President Toda said, "When giving guidance to members, it is important that you explain things in a convincing manner." When members truly understand and accept your guidance, they will move forward of their own accord.

Our organization will reach a deadlock if leaders simply give orders or lapse into a bureaucratic mind-set.

When one member gains firm conviction and stands up to take action, fresh waves of development are set in motion. I would like to ask the youth division leaders to exercise outstanding leadership for victory, acting with courage and sincerity, in their respective places of mission.

WHEN YOU STRIVE IN FAITH, EARNESTLY DETERMINED TO TAKE FULL RESPONSIBILITY, BOUNDLESS WISDOM WILL WELL UP FROM WITHIN YOU.

14

STRIVING TO ACHIEVE THE GOAL OF PEACE

Peace does not exist in some distant place. It begins with us. It starts with becoming friends with another person.

Youth have always been the ones sacrificed in war. That's why it's crucial for youth to strive vigorously for peace, for you to forge a growing network of youth committed to peace. I would like you, my friends, with the power of youth, to create a society free from the brutality of war, a world where everyone can feel glad to have been born and enjoy a happy life.

Peace is something that we must strive for and achieve. Kosen-rufu is nothing other than the highest expression of peace.

Nichiren Daishonin writes, "All people have the Buddha nature" (WND-1, 756). Everyone possesses the supremely noble life state of Buddhahood. Respecting one another is the truest way to peace. That's why it's so important for young people to share this great life-affirming philosophy of Nichiren Buddhism with other youth.

• • •

First Soka Gakkai president Tsunesaburo Makiguchi, who resisted the demands of the oppressive militarist authorities during World War II, died in prison for his beliefs. Second Soka Gakkai president Josei Toda, who was imprisoned alongside Mr. Makiguchi, pledged after his release to vindicate his deceased mentor. He stood up alone amid the postwar devastation and initiated a great struggle for peace.

Carrying on the spirit of these two great mentors, I fought resolutely against the devilish nature of authority. I have built bridges of friendship throughout the globe and expanded a network for peace, culture, and education to bring people closer together.

To thoroughly treasure each person and steadfastly battle devilish functions that would cause people to suffer—this is the spirit of Soka mentors and disciples committed to the cause of peace.

* * *

Nichiren warned that the reason for the warfare and suffering that plagued his time was that the power of the people was weak (see WND-1, 1134).

The only way to bring an end to war is for ordinary people to become strong and wise. It is vital that people around the world unite solidly in purpose.

That's why I call on you, the youth, to be strong and strive in harmony with good friends, and for you to be wise and discerning by always basing your lives on the sound philosophy of Nichiren Buddhism.

While courageously tackling the immediate problems in your lives, please tenaciously continue to challenge your human revolution.

Chant, study, speak with others, take action, strive earnestly, and keep pressing forward triumphantly for the sake of your own happiness and that of others, for the prosperity of society and the land in which you live, and for peace throughout the entire world.

15

TAKING ONE BRAVE STEP FORWARD FOR KOSEN-RUFU

Youth is a struggle, as is life. In any endeavor, taking the initiative is key. As the Japanese saying goes, "Seize the initiative and you will win."

Failing to take the initiative at the right moment can lead to defeat. Seizing the initiative is the sure way to victory.

Give full attention to even the smallest matters. Always promptly take the appropriate measures in any situation.

Each sensitive and earnest action taken for the members' happiness and for the success of our movement spreads joy. Kosen-rufu gains momentum through the passion, encouragement, and swift responses of leaders.

• • •

As I engaged in every struggle, I told my mentor: "Please do not worry. I will succeed! I will win without fail!" And I always kept my promise.

In any undertaking, victory goes to those who are firmly

determined to win. That's why it's important to focus our minds on winning no matter what. If we chant with this kind of resolve, then courage and wisdom will well forth from within us. Our lives will shine brightly and vibrantly.

Nichiren Daishonin writes, "Employ the strategy of the Lotus Sutra before any other" (WND-1, 1001). Chant powerfully and advance with courage, perseverance, and fortitude.

Overconfidence and carelessness will lead to failure. Those who fully exert themselves to the very end with dedication and determination will be victorious. This is an unchanging rule.

• • •

We all have areas in our lives that we haven't challenged. The more courageously you take action for kosen-rufu with the spirit of youth, the more you will be able to open new frontiers for our movement.

Nothing is sadder than a youth that passes without any record of achievement. Take one brave step forward for kosen-rufu. The efforts you make now will open a new era in which you will take the lead. Create a personal history of which you can proudly say, "I opened the way to this victory!"

There is no obstacle that the youth of the SGI cannot break through. Joyfully achieve one resounding victory after another!

16

PERSEVERANCE IS STRENGTH

Friendship is life's treasure. Nothing is more beautiful than friendship. The spirit of friendship and Buddhist humanism are one.

Let's open our hearts, greet others brightly, and be sincere in our interactions. Through our own thoughtful conduct, we can deepen our friendships and spread trust.

Sincerity is the only way to truly reach and win people's hearts. Always be courteous, speak clearly, and keep your promises. Such seemingly small things lead to success.

Let's treasure our ties with good friends. Mr. Toda stressed the importance of extending a hand of friendship to people when they experience hard or challenging times. Let's always take pride in being true and loyal friends.

• • •

Meet and talk with someone each day. Even if you just talk with one person, then in three years' time, you'll have spoken with more than a thousand people! Persevere, day after day. Make steady, persistent efforts. It is truly a case of

"Perseverance is strength."

All of your efforts are a source of growth. The unseen efforts you make for the sake of kosen-rufu, in particular, will return to you as your own benefit. Nothing is wasted. Unseen virtue brings about brilliant visible reward (see WND-1, 940).

Nichiren Daishonin writes, "To have faith like water means to believe continuously without ever regressing" (WND-1, 899). Those who advance steadily and persistently on their chosen path will triumph in the end.

• • •

The key to fostering capable individuals is encouragement.

Without encouragement, it can be difficult for people to take a fresh step forward. Let's sincerely encourage each person, lift each person's spirit, and enable each person to forge ahead with a bright, upbeat spirit.

Mr. Toda said that "capable individuals" are not some special category of people but are developed through being trained and fostered.

Let's support people when they are struggling or suffering. Knowing that someone cares will be a source of strength for them. Such warm concern builds a network of beautiful friendship.

Nichiren writes, "One is the mother of ten thousand" (WND-1, 131). Even wholeheartedly encouraging one person has the potential to bring forth the power of ten thousand.

17

BUDDHISM IS MANIFESTED IN OUR ACTIONS

Let's create fresh momentum! I hope you'll begin by striving vigorously yourself. Please set an example through what you yourself have achieved and challenged. When youth take the lead, it lightens people's hearts and imparts courage.

At the same time, it is important that leaders shine the spotlight on each of our dedicated members and offer warm words of appreciation and praise. Wholeheartedly treasure those who are striving the hardest, and do everything you can to encourage them. This will bring everyone even more joy.

In addition, let's be sure to express heartfelt appreciation to the families who offer their homes for SGI activities and be polite and considerate when holding meetings there.

Nichiren Daishonin writes, "The purpose of the appearance in this world of Shakyamuni Buddha, the lord of teachings, lies in his behavior as a human being" (WND-1, 852). Always keep in mind that our true measure as a practitioner of Nichiren Buddhism is revealed in our sincere and considerate actions.

• • •

Nothing is more refreshing than the warm, enthusiastic greetings and expressions of thanks of young people.

President Toda used to say that what's important for youth is not fame or status or money; it is trust. The first step to winning people's trust is a pleasant greeting.

When I was young, I did my best to greet everyone at work cheerfully. Doing so invigorated my entire workplace.

I also went out of my way to greet the residents in my apartment building and neighbors on the street. The sound of a lively greeting can expand our circle of trust and friendship in the community and society at large.

• • •

During our pioneering campaigns to propagate this Buddhism in Osaka and Yamaguchi, it was mainly new members who strove alongside me to leave behind a golden record of victory.

Today, a steady stream of new members and freshly inspired capable people are emerging throughout the world. Nothing could make me happier.

The times are growing increasingly troubled. Organizations that can foster new capable people will triumph. Toward that end, I hope all of you, the members of the youth division, will achieve new, golden victories on the noble stage of your personal mission.

18

LEADING A BRILLIANT LIFE TOGETHER WITH THE SGI

In the depths of our beings, we have the strength to withstand every form of hardship, the underlying power to overcome them without fail. Nichiren Daishonin showed us this through his own example, and the SGI, following in his footsteps, has triumphed over all obstacles.

In *The Record of the Orally Transmitted Teachings*, Nichiren Daishonin says, "As long as they [my followers] are together with Nichiren, they will reach the treasure land" (OTT, 78).

When we advance together with the SGI, the organization directly connected to the Daishonin, we can win in every situation. As we continue striving to transform any and all karmic challenges, let us fulfill our great vow for kosen-rufu.

• • •

Associating with good friends is crucial to attaining Buddhahood. Having wonderful fellow members is a joy beyond compare. I hope you will connect with seniors and fellow members in faith who you know to be honest and true and who inspire you. At the same time, please strive to become a positive companion who imparts courage and hope to all those around you.

Like-minded friends are those who share the same aspirations. The SGI is the ultimate gathering of like-minded friends, with a common aim and resolve as Bodhisattvas of the Earth.

As SGI members, we share joys and sorrows and warmly encourage one another as we dedicate our lives to realizing kosen-rufu and establishing the correct teaching for the peace of the land. Always remember that the heritage of faith flows in the organization whose members are moving forward along this correct path in life and are solidly united in the spirit of "many in body, one in mind."

• • •

Leadership positions in the SGI are noble "positions of responsibility." Therefore, I'd like for leaders to value each member and do their utmost to ensure that every activity for kosen-rufu is a success.

A profound sense of responsibility gives rise to deep prayer. It is crucial that those in positions of responsibility vanquish all devilish functions with the lion's roar of Nam-myoho-renge-kyo and protect the members.

Especially when the momentum for kosen-rufu accelerates, it's important that, through chanting powerfully and paying careful attention to detail, you take leadership to ensure that there are no accidents or mishaps. When your prayers and actions are in rhythm, you will be able to achieve breakthroughs for victory.

I would like you, my beloved successors, to protect and contribute to the further development of our organization, which President Toda described as being more precious to him than his own life.

Together with the Mystic Law, the SGI, and your fellow members, please adorn your youth with brilliant victory!

19

LET'S HOLD MEETINGS THAT INSPIRE EVERYONE

SGI meetings are assemblies of Buddhas, gatherings of Bodhisattvas of the Earth, dedicated to advancing kosen-rufu.

My mentor never took even the smallest meeting lightly; he always approached each one with a serious attitude. He poured his heart and soul into each gathering, thinking: "Everything begins with the members who attend this meeting. We will achieve victory from this meeting."

It's important that leaders and all those helping organize meetings chant earnestly and prepare thoroughly so that participants will feel truly glad they came. I hope leaders will brim with vitality and encourage members so they will be motivated to strive their utmost. This will inspire everyone to take a step forward and create the momentum for opening a new era.

• • •

Some of you may have a hard time speaking in front of others, but there's no need to feel compelled to sound clever or eloquent. Nichiren writes, "Words echo the thoughts of the mind and find expression through the voice" (WND-2, 843). The important thing is to convey your thoughts with sincerity in a way that truly resonates in your listeners' hearts.

There's no need to put on airs—just be who you are. Convey your great passion for kosen-rufu in your own way, honestly and sincerely. Share your personal experiences in faith in a straightforward way. Strive to lighten the members' hearts and impart courage. If members feel "I could do that too!" they will be able to fully demonstrate their abilities with confidence.

Since the time of our organization's founder, Tsunesaburo Makiguchi, the Soka Gakkai has forged unity through dialogue that helps members gain a deeper understanding of our movement.

Pressuring and coercing members won't inspire them to take action. Drawing forth the heartfelt accord "Yes, that's it!" will move them to act on their own initiative.

As leaders, please make sure that you speak to members in a way that is clear, concrete, and easy to understand, so that everyone can devote themselves to activities with complete assurance.

To do this, it's crucial that you chant Nam-myoho-renge-kyo and bring forth wisdom based on the principle of substituting faith for wisdom. Let's draw out and pool everyone's wisdom. The key to victory in advancing kosen-rufu is creating a solidly united gathering of self-motivated individuals.

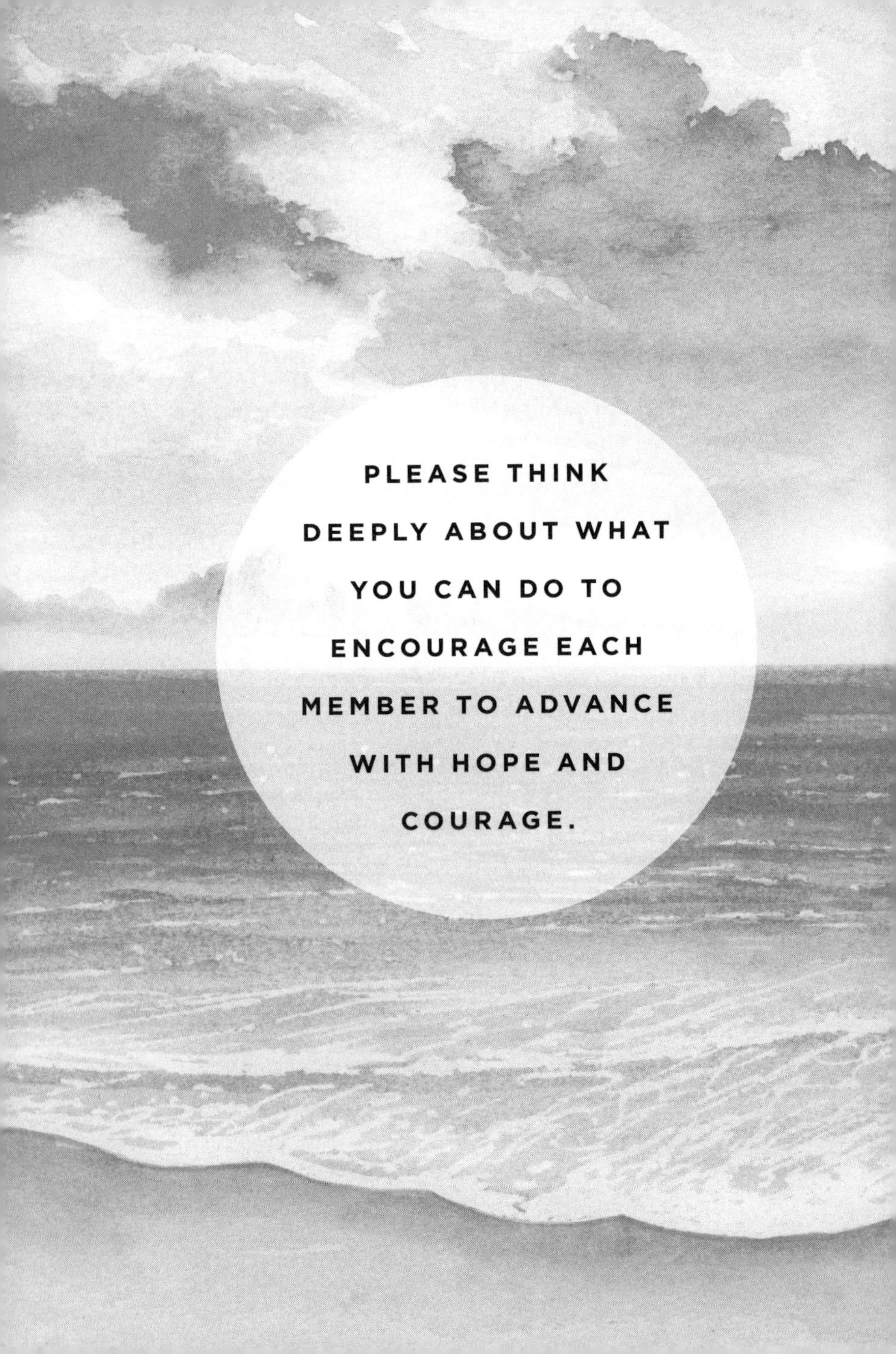

PLEASE THINK DEEPLY ABOUT WHAT YOU CAN DO TO ENCOURAGE EACH MEMBER TO ADVANCE WITH HOPE AND COURAGE.

20

CREATE A STEADY STREAM OF CAPABLE PEOPLE

We need to search out and foster new capable people. It's important that we encourage and help them develop their abilities.

Each member is a noble Bodhisattva of the Earth. Please find everyone's strong points and praise each one. Let's ensure that all members can make the most of their unique qualities to contribute to kosen-rufu.

As leaders, please avoid judging others based on your own narrow-minded criteria. More importantly, please don't let personal likes and dislikes influence you. If you care only for those you get along with, truly capable people will not develop.

President Makiguchi compared finding and fostering capable people to "panning for gold."

Our organization has created a stream of golden capable people through members taking active part in SGI activities. Indeed, this is the best way to foster capable people.

• • •

Those in vice-leadership positions are the key to unity. Let's ensure that their role and mission are clearly defined. When they can carry out their specific responsibilities and engage in activities, the organization will continue to grow limitlessly.

There may be cases where your juniors are appointed to central leadership positions. In such situations, I hope you will steadfastly support them with a spirit of deep generosity based on faith.

Both the central and vice leaders need to unite in spirit, chanting to the Gohonzon so that they can bring forth their abilities and advance kosen-rufu. If they respect one another and cooperate, they can set the wheels in motion toward victory. Joy and benefit will also spread throughout the organization.

• • •

Nichiren Daishonin writes to his youthful follower Nanjo Tokimitsu, "Teaching another something is the same as oiling the wheels of a cart so that they turn even though it [the cart] is heavy, or as floating a boat on water so that it moves ahead easily" (WND-1, 1086).

As leaders, please think deeply about what you can do to encourage each member to advance with hope and courage. Then take the necessary steps to do so.

Just giving guidance without putting yourself in the members' shoes isn't very meaningful. It's important that you listen to them, chant with them, open their hearts, and truly understand their situations.

Doing everything you can to empower all members to exercise their abilities to the fullest and advance cheerfully with pride and conviction is what makes you a true leader of Nichiren Buddhism.

21

CONTINUE WINNING THROUGH PERSEVERANCE

How we begin each day is crucial. Let's start off the morning with the vigor of the rising sun. Doing gongyo and chanting Nam-myoho-renge-kyo awakens and revitalizes our lives.

The busier we get and the greater the challenges we face, the more important it is for us to win in the morning. Please create a record of victory in your youth by winning each morning.

The historic Osaka Campaign of 1956 also began with chanting vigorously each morning. That's how we could make the impossible possible. We achieved a monumental victory that will shine for eternity.

When we engage in a struggle for kosen-rufu, the three obstacles and four devils will invariably arise to assail us. Every day is an earnest challenge. That's why it's essential that we chant powerfully.

Through employing the strategy of the Lotus Sutra—chanting Nam-myoho-renge-kyo—let's strive to transform even opponents into allies for our movement.

• • •

Momentum is key to winning in every struggle for kosen-rufu. The inner determination of leaders is the force that increases this momentum.

First, as leaders, are you striving with a momentum driven by a firm determination to succeed? It's important that you brim with an unwavering resolve to triumph without fail.

Second, are you advancing with the momentum to refute the erroneous and reveal the true? I hope a passionate spirit of justice and truth will burn brightly in your hearts.

Third, are you forging ahead with the powerful, lion-like momentum of mentor and disciple? Please advance with the spirit of the oneness of mentor and disciple, confidently sharing Nichiren Buddhism with others.

Fourth, are you progressing with dynamic, unified momentum that will open the way to unceasing victory? Please show people throughout the world the underlying strength of Soka through the unity of "many in body, one in mind."

• • •

Everything is constantly changing. Our Buddhist practice enables us to steer those changes in a positive direction—the direction of happiness.

People can always change for the better. We can also change our environment for the better.

The Lotus Sutra teaches that the Buddha transformed the land three times, turning it into a pure land (see LSOC,

212–13). Kosen-rufu is the great struggle to carry out such a transformation in our environment and turn the troubled saha world in which we live into a Buddha land, a realm of happiness and peace. As such, instead of lamenting challenging situations, let's rouse the strong determination to change them.

It took Shakyamuni repeated times before the land was fully transformed. Therefore, let's always keep in mind that only by chanting wholeheartedly and persevering in our efforts for kosen-rufu can we positively transform our communities.

22

ENACT A BRILLIANT DRAMA OF HUMAN REVOLUTION

Youth is a constant struggle against problems and worries. Because you are advancing, challenges arise. Experiencing problems and sufferings enables you to grow.

In *The Record of the Orally Transmitted Teachings*, Nichiren Daishonin speaks of "burning the firewood of earthly desires, summoning up the wisdom fire of bodhi or enlightenment" (OTT, 11). In other words, we do not seek to extinguish sufferings but instead use them as fuel to make the "flames of wisdom" of human revolution burn brightly. The driving force for achieving this is chanting Nam-myoho-renge-kyo.

The Mystic Law gives us the strength to live out our lives and is the wellspring of happiness. It provides the strength to triumph, no matter our circumstances. That is why it is important that we chant wholeheartedly to the Gohonzon and challenge our problems with courage and hope.

• • •

When I was young, I worked tirelessly from morning to night to support my mentor, Josei Toda, whose businesses were in serious financial trouble. There were days I returned to my apartment completely exhausted and collapsed without even being able to remove my shoes.

But because I continued challenging myself, I could open the way forward. Thanks to those efforts, I became who I am today. I also became very healthy.

Nichiren Daishonin writes, "The wise will rejoice while the foolish will retreat" (WND-1, 637).

The lives of youth who strive with courage and joy toward lofty goals are radiant. You may be extremely busy. There may be no end to your struggles. But I hope your spirit will always shine with pride and confidence, no matter what trying challenges you face. Therein lies the genuine victory of youth.

• • •

We are noble Bodhisattvas of the Earth who have appeared in this world for the sake of kosen-rufu. Living in a corrupt and troubled age, we have the greatest possible mission to propagate the Buddhist teaching of respect for the dignity of life and to dedicate ourselves to the realization of peace and happiness of all humankind.

The Japanese word for *mission* means "to use one's life." For what purpose should you use your precious young lives? Every day that you chant Nam-myoho-renge-kyo and use your lives to work for the welfare of others, your community, and society, you proceed along the most positive path of life in rhythm with the universe.

No matter what adversities may beset you, you can definitely change poison into medicine and carry out your human revolution. And by transforming karma into mission, you will be able to encourage and help guide many others.

23

TRUST IS A TREASURE FOR YOUTH

The trustworthy will win. For young people, even if they possess nothing else, the trust of others is an invaluable treasure.

President Toda said: "Keeping one's promises is the basis for gaining others' trust. If you can't fulfill a request, you should say so clearly. But once you agree to take something on, it's important that you make every possible effort to follow through."

In accord with my mentor's guidance, I always did my best to keep every promise I made, no matter how small. As a result, trust grew, flowers of friendship blossomed, and a great network for peace came to fruition around the globe.

Never forget that worldwide kosen-rufu advances through heart-to-heart connections.

• • •

I hope you will have the courage to seek advice when you need it. There are times when it is important to consult with others rather than struggle alone. Seeking advice is nothing to be ashamed of. In fact, being willing to open your heart can be a truly valuable asset.

In both your work and your Buddhist practice, if you rely solely on your own judgment, it is easy to become attached to your own point of view or be swayed by your environment.

President Toda stressed the importance of having people, or even just one person, you can talk to about your true feelings and turn to for advice—people who can offer you fresh insights. Such individuals will be an important source of support and strength.

The pride and tradition of the SGI is to nurture beautiful, warm, family-like ties, creating an environment where members can ask one another anything and confide straightforwardly about their struggles and doubts.

* * *

Promoting understanding for our movement requires above all courage, patience, and sincerity. When you summon the courage to meet with people and sincerely talk with them at length, your words will resonate in their hearts.

The Lotus Sutra describes the Bodhisattvas of the Earth as follows:

> They are clever at difficult questions and answers,
> their minds know no fear.
> They have firmly cultivated persevering minds,
> upright in dignity and virtue. (LSOC, 263)

My young friends, fellow Bodhisattvas of the Earth! Your lives are endowed with this tremendous power of conversation. Do not worry if you aren't eloquent speakers. Every effort you make to share the ideals of the SGI with others is part of your training for becoming champions of dialogue. I hope you will boldly and freely engage in such efforts, reaching out to talk with one person after another, thereby promoting greater understanding for our movement.

Those who are sincere are certain to win out in the end. Kosen-rufu is the process of demonstrating that through our own actions.

24

ENCOURAGING ONE ANOTHER AND ADVANCING TOGETHER

The key to dialogue is listening. Listening is learning; it expands our world. If we interact with others with respect and sincerity, conversation will naturally flow. Dialogue is the way to achieve real heart-to-heart communication.

An ancient philosopher said the reason we have two ears is so we may listen twice as much as we speak.

Sometimes just having someone listen can dispel your worries and concerns. Or when you share a problem with someone, the answer may become clear as you talk about it.

Conversation has the wondrous power to elevate its participants to a new and higher plane—that's why listening intently to someone is in itself a great form of encouragement.

• • •

Showing all who dedicate themselves to kosen-rufu the same respect one would a Buddha—this is the foremost message of the Lotus Sutra (see OTT, 192). When we praise those striving for kosen-rufu, we gain benefit ourselves and help others do the same.

As Nichiren Daishonin writes: "When praised highly by others, one feels that there is no hardship one cannot bear. Such is the courage that springs from words of praise" (WND-1, 385).

As leaders, it is important not to overlook those who are working hard behind the scenes. Be keenly aware of even the smallest efforts they are making and praise them. Impart hope and motivation.

I hope you will help draw forth each person's unique qualities and work together with everyone in a spirit of mutual respect. Such teamwork will lead to solid development.

• • •

When someone is struggling, read Nichiren's writings with them, chant to the Gohonzon with them, and take a step forward together with them. Empathizing with the struggles of others and chanting with them will also give you the strength to overcome your own problems. Those who encourage one another will flourish and triumph together.

Referring to the way plants coexist harmoniously in nature, the Daishonin writes, "Even insentient plants and trees share as one a friend's joys and sorrows" (WND-2, 964).

When we encounter especially difficult obstacles, let's encourage one another even more cheerfully and positively. In precisely such trying times, let's courageously take on each challenge, uniting to overcome them one by one. That is our role as fellow members in faith and the purpose of our Buddhist practice.

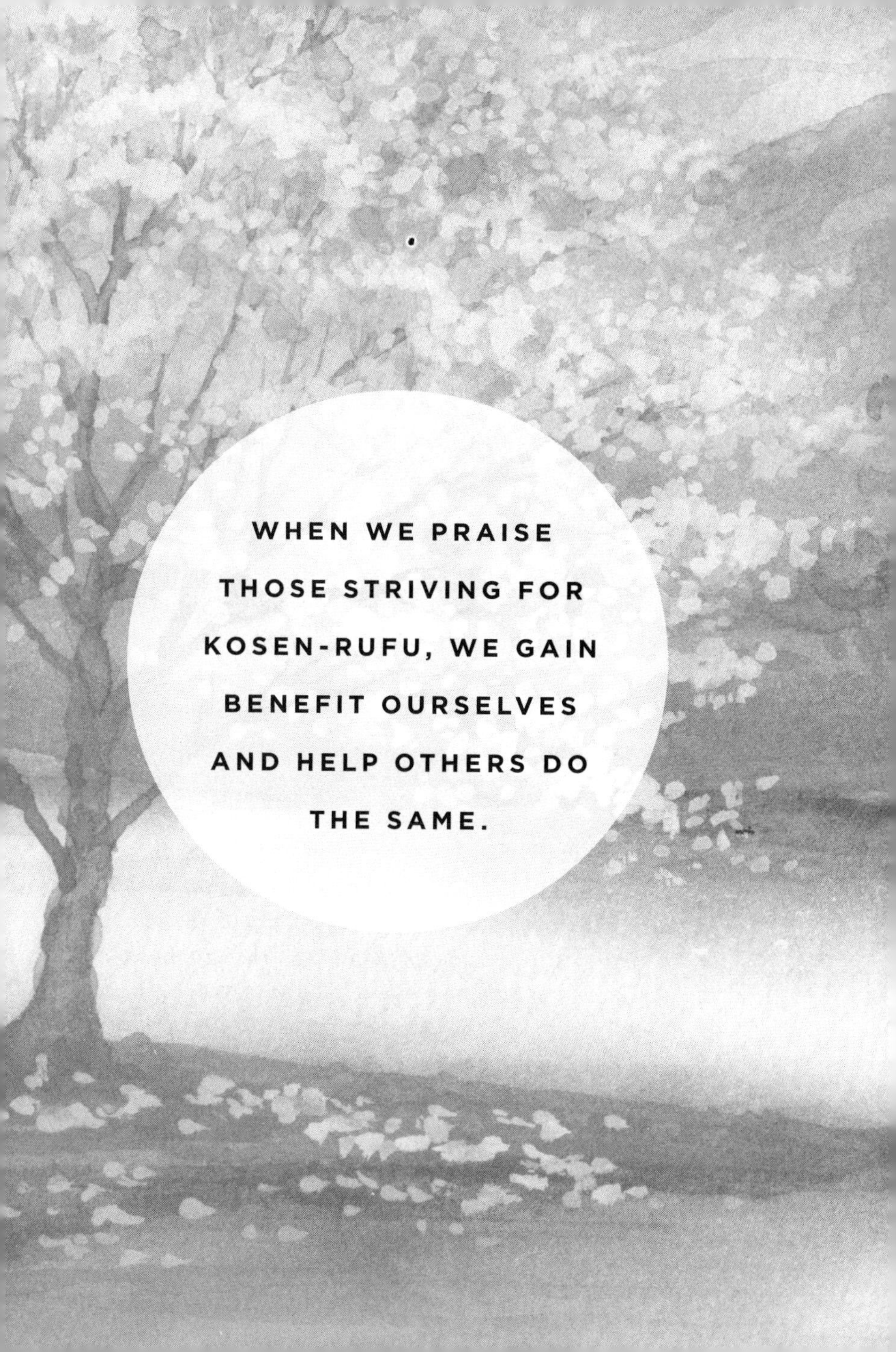
WHEN WE PRAISE THOSE STRIVING FOR KOSEN-RUFU, WE GAIN BENEFIT OURSELVES AND HELP OTHERS DO THE SAME.

25

STRIVE AS FOREMOST CHAMPIONS OF PHILOSOPHY

Today, there is an absence of philosophy and a lack of principles. Few can speak with confidence about life, society, and the ideals that might best support them.

Nichiren Daishonin writes: "This [Lotus] sutra is superior to all other sutras. It is like the lion king, the monarch of all the creatures that run on the ground, and like the eagle, the king of all the creatures that fly in the sky" (WND-1, 929–30).

Priding itself on being the foremost champion in the realm of philosophy, the SGI has been illuminating the world with the philosophy that respects the dignity of all life.

Kosen-rufu is a struggle of words. Members of the youth division must not let lies and false assertions prevail. Please continue speaking with others about peace, justice, and happiness, touching and awakening the lives of one youth after another.

• • •

Let us advance with unflagging courage. Nichiren Daishonin declares, "Those with the heart of a lion king are sure to attain Buddhahood" (WND-1, 302). The "heart of a lion king" is another name for unsurpassed courage, a courage that fears nothing.

Life is a struggle. Therefore, please resolutely chant Nam-myoho-renge-kyo and take a decisive, courageous step forward. The heart of a lion king cannot be defeated by any suffering or hardship. It will always overcome them. Each time you win with the heart of a lion king, you grow as a person. Avoiding struggles, however, limits one's growth. As young people, I hope you will boldly and energetically transform difficulty into joy and obstacles into fuel for self-development.

* * *

Speak out courageously and without hesitation for your beliefs! Nothing is more refreshing and inspiring than young people confidently sharing their views. You don't have to worry about being eloquent. The truth itself is powerful.

In *The Record of the Orally Transmitted Teachings*, the Daishonin states: "The first *shi* of the word *shishi*, or 'lion' [which means 'teacher'], is the Wonderful Law that is passed on by the teacher. The second *shi* [which means 'child'] is the Wonderful Law as it is received by the disciples. The 'roar' [of the term 'lion's roar' (*shishi ku*)] is the sound of the teacher and the disciples chanting in unison" (OTT, 111).

The essence of the lion's roar is the mentor and disciple speaking out for truth, united in spirit, to advance kosen-rufu. The first three Soka Gakkai presidents, sharing the bonds of mentor and disciple, all triumphed because they spoke out fearlessly in this way.

Now it's time for you, the members of the youth division, to take center stage. Speak out with courage and raise high the banner of victory and honor!

26

BE AMBASSADORS OF SOKA!

The spirit of youth is courage. Being sharp-witted, bold, and exuberant are hallmarks of youth.

President Toda appointed me as the first head of our organization's public relations department when I was only twenty-six. He even entrusted me with meeting and negotiating with important leaders in society, saying, "Daisaku, you take care of it!"

Representing my mentor, I met with many people and forged new ties of trust. I also spoke out firmly against those who slandered and criticized Mr. Toda and the Soka Gakkai. I confidently let everyone know about the true greatness of my mentor and our organization. I regard those days with great pride.

The more we meet and talk with people, the more it will come back to us as a source of strength. It will adorn our lives with great good fortune.

I now entrust everything to you, the members of the youth division. Striving with the spirit that you represent the SGI, please write a fresh page of history and open new horizons in our movement for kosen-rufu.

Nichiren Daishonin writes, "I entrust you with the propagation of Buddhism in your province" (WND-1, 1117). When we are actively engaged in our communities, we can sow the seeds of happiness by helping many others form a connection to Buddhism.

As emissaries of the Buddha, our voices do the Buddha's work. Speaking with others is also the heart of the Daishonin's ideal of "establishing the correct teaching for the peace of the land."

Interacting with many different kinds of people and engaging them in discussion enables you to break out of your shell and develop a bigger state of life. Even if you may not be a very good speaker, there is no need to worry. Just keep challenging yourself. Talking to others about Buddhism is the shortest route for carrying out your human revolution.

* * *

Kosen-rufu is all about making friends.

In a number of his writings, Nichiren Daishonin cites the following passage from the Lotus Sutra: "Although the devil and the devil's people will be there, they will all protect the Buddhist Law" (LSOC, 145). The aim of our effort to spread understanding for our movement is to turn even opponents into allies.

I hope that you, the members of the youth division, will speak with others confidently and frankly as fellow human beings, no matter who they may be. All you need do is share your convictions in a polite, pleasant, unaffected, and natural way.

Nothing makes a deeper impression than the sincerity of youth. Such sincerity will inspire trust and understanding.

27

BE PEOPLE WHO CONTRIBUTE TO PEACE

Nichiren Daishonin writes, "One day of life is more valuable than all the treasures of the major world system" (WND-1, 955).

There is no treasure in the universe more precious than life. That's why we must never, for any reason, cause harm to others or ourselves. As SGI members, let us continue our efforts to make the Buddhist principle of supreme respect for the dignity of life the universal spirit of the age.

Humanity has suffered greatly from its repeated history of violence and war. As SGI members, we are striving wherever we are to transform the destiny of humankind through discussions based on the Daishonin's ideal of "establishing the correct teaching for the peace of the land" and through our activities for peace.

Thinkers the world over have high hopes for our work. Now is the time for you, our youth division members, to take your place on the global stage with pride and confidence.

• • •

Concrete action is more important than the most high-sounding theories.

Peace is not something removed from our daily lives. It starts with being firmly rooted in our communities and treasuring each individual. Developing heart-to-heart bonds with others where we are right now—by opening our hearts, acting in friendship, and using our wisdom—is the surest way to build peace.

We are living in an age of globalization. If you, the members of the youth division, can create a hope-filled model of human harmony in your local communities through your united efforts, it will have a ripple effect throughout the entire world.

• • •

War cruelly robs young people of their lives and destroys their youth. As a disciple of Josei Toda, I have striven with the determination to prevent future generations from experiencing such tragedy.

The only way to vanquish the demonic force of war is for each individual to carry out human revolution and build an indestructible fortress of peace within. It is vital to rally the passion and energy of youth and expand our great movement for peace, culture, and education.

Nothing—not even nuclear weapons—is stronger than the power of truth and good that resides in the human heart.

I hope, therefore, that you will make your own young lives and those of others shine as you expand your network of friendship and trust, starting with where you are now.

28

THE PASSION AND ENERGY OF YOUTH WILL OPEN A NEW ERA

In every age, it is the passion and power of youth that has changed the times and created history.

Amid the devastation of postwar Japan, second Soka Gakkai president Josei Toda resolved to realize a peaceful society and called forth the "young flag bearers" who would strive alongside him to spearhead the movement for kosen-rufu.

Kosen-rufu is achieved through the emergence of a steady stream of youthful Bodhisattvas of the Earth. There is no more meaningful endeavor to which one can dedicate one's youth. I hope that each of you, the youth division members, will during your youth joyfully strive to leave behind a lasting positive legacy where you are carrying out your mission—a legacy of which you can be proud.

We have truly entered a wondrous time when young people all around the world are standing up with a great vow for kosen-rufu. My friends of the youth division, it is your turn to take the lead!

• • •

Faith in the Mystic Law is the engine that will propel you in the direction of happiness.

Strong faith enables you to strengthen your life force and gain indestructible happiness, no matter what happens. It empowers you to achieve victory in life without fail and to lead your family and descendants toward happiness.

It is important that you pray "as earnestly as though to produce fire from damp wood, or to obtain water from parched ground" (WND-1, 444) and also "pray intently that Shakyamuni, Many Treasures, and the Buddhas of the ten directions will all gather and take possession of your body to assist you" (WND-1, 829).

The essence of faith is to summon within your lives the protective functions of the universe so that you can display the power and wisdom of the Buddha.

• • •

Even in the arts or academia, the teacher-student or mentor-disciple relationship depends on the commitment of the student or disciple. When disciples in the realm of Buddhism stand up with a commitment to carry on their mentor's teachings and make their mentor's spirit their own, the same courage as their mentor will surge forth from within them.

Everything is determined by the disciples. The efforts of the disciples create the appropriate time for fresh expansion in the movement for kosen-rufu.

Now is the time to awaken to your unsurpassed mission

and proudly expand the network of capable young people dedicated to truth and justice!

With the passion and power of youth, please build an indestructible, ever-victorious bastion of Soka that will triumph and flourish eternally!

29

FOREVER COMMITTED TO SPREADING THE MYSTIC LAW

Nichiren Daishonin writes, "Those who become Nichiren's disciples and lay believers should realize the profound karmic relationship they share with him and spread the Lotus Sutra [Nam-myoho-renge-kyo] as he does" (WND-1, 994).

We are Bodhisattvas of the Earth who have chosen to be born at this time because of our wish to carry out kosen-rufu together. When we chant Nam-myoho-renge-kyo with an awareness of our profound mission and karmic connection, infinite strength and wisdom will surge forth from within us.

Spreading the Mystic Law is the foremost action of a Buddha. So let's joyfully and positively challenge ourselves in this endeavor.

• • •

Sharing Nichiren Buddhism is a noble undertaking in which we show utmost respect for and sincerely encourage each person.

There are times when our words, no matter how well

intentioned, do not reach the other person. We may have bad or bitter experiences. But all such efforts are transformed into treasures for our lives.

Nichiren Buddhism is the Buddhism of sowing. With even a single word, we can plant the seed of Buddhahood in another person's life. Such a seed, once planted, will someday definitely sprout, blossom, and bear fruit.

Because our members have tirelessly planted the seeds of the Mystic Law again and again wherever they went, a great forest of kosen-rufu has flourished around the world.

People are eagerly seeking Buddhism today. Therefore, I want you, the youth, to press ahead with courage, speaking with others and sharing your beliefs.

• • •

Faith in Nichiren Buddhism is the driving force for our lives and the wellspring of happiness. Those who strive hard in SGI activities for themselves and others brim with energy and vitality. Their happiness is assured.

Sharing Nichiren Buddhism with others is a challenge, but there is no greater cause for growth. It is putting into action the Buddhist principle of earthly desires leading to enlightenment. The more you exert yourselves out of your desire to help others, the happier you will become. This is because struggling to share Nichiren Buddhism with others is, in itself, the struggle of a Buddha. Those who share Nichiren Buddhism, therefore, already manifest the life state of Buddhahood.

President Toda's novel, *The Human Revolution,* ends with the main character proclaiming his firm determination while in prison for his beliefs: "I will spend my life spreading this noble teaching of the Lotus Sutra [Nam-myoho-renge-kyo]!" This is the essence of the Soka Gakkai spirit.

My youthful successors, with the unshakable conviction that you are Buddhas and entities of the Mystic Law, please use your voices unsparingly to spread the great philosophy of Nichiren Buddhism!

30

BASE YOURSELVES ON THE FOREMOST PHILOSOPHY OF LIFE

Nichiren Daishonin writes, "Without practice and study, there can be no Buddhism" (WND-1, 386). It is an SGI tradition, especially for the youth, to strive in the "two ways of practice and study" (WND-1, 386), making every possible effort to do so.

When we study Nichiren's writings, immeasurable wisdom and indomitable courage well forth. It powerfully revitalizes us.

Studying the Daishonin's teachings gives us the strength to win over ourselves and our karma and to win in life and society. Even if it is just a sentence or paragraph each day, let's engrave Nichiren's writings in our hearts and strive to put them into practice in our lives.

• • •

Among the Daishonin's writings that Mr. Toda instructed me to study in depth was "The Actions of the Votary of the

Lotus Sutra." In it, we find Nichiren's dauntless declaration immediately before the Tatsunokuchi Persecution: "How amusing! Look at Hei no Saemon gone mad! You gentlemen have just toppled the pillar of Japan" (WND-1, 766).

Buddhist study based on the spirit of Soka mentor and disciple enables us to summon up this invincible courage of a lion king and press forward in our struggle for kosen-rufu.

When we gain a correct understanding of the principles of Nichiren Buddhism, we will not be swayed at a crucial moment. Using the bright mirror of Buddhism, we will be able to clearly see the onslaughts of devilish functions for what they are. Study builds a strong framework for maintaining our Buddhist practice throughout our lives.

• • •

What makes a person truly admirable? It is neither social status nor fame but rather the ideals and philosophy they embrace and practice.

Nichiren writes, "If the Law that one embraces is supreme, then the person who embraces it must accordingly be foremost among all others" (WND-1, 61).

Nichiren Buddhism, which teaches the universal dignity of life and the path to lasting happiness and peace for all humanity, is the highest ideal and foremost philosophy. And young people who study and spread this Buddhism are, accordingly, the foremost people whose lives are crowned with supreme honor.

The times are seeking a sound philosophy. My friends of the youth division, please become people of great wisdom who brim with happiness and victory, and brightly illuminate the hearts of your friends with the teachings of hope.

31

CHANGING POISON INTO MEDICINE THROUGH FAITH

Life's course does not always proceed smoothly. There are days of deep sadness and times of great suffering. It is only to be expected, then, that young people who have taken on a noble mission will face many hardships.

But the deeper the sorrow and the greater the hardships we face, the more profound our joy will be when we overcome them.

We practice Nichiren Buddhism, which enables us to change poison into medicine. Nichiren Daishonin writes, "Misfortune will change into fortune" (WND-1, 412).

We can transform all our problems and sufferings, moving everything in a positive direction—in the direction of happiness, human revolution, and Buddhahood without fail. With the passage of time, this will become clear.

Nothing is ever wasted in Buddhism. Times of adversity are opportunities to expand our state of life and accumulate benefit.

• • •

Let's press forward with powerful optimism especially in times of difficulty. Bewailing our circumstances will not change anything. Looking back will not get us anywhere. The first thing to do is chant. Everything is contained in chanting Nam-myoho-renge-kyo.

Life is a struggle to the very end. That is why it is important that we chant with the determination to win no matter what.

Faith in the Mystic Law is a source of limitless hope and self-confidence. Even though we may be in the midst of hellish suffering, the power of chanting enables us to turn our environment into the Land of Tranquil Light.

Please stand up based on faith, come what may.

• • •

Your present struggles will become the firm foundation for developing your lives into an indestructible fortress. Rather than strategizing or taking shortcuts, I hope you will entrust everything to the Gohonzon and challenge yourselves with courage and perseverance.

The Hall of the Great Vow for Kosen-rufu that SGI members have been waiting for will soon be completed (in November 2013). It is a magnificent citadel bequeathed to the youth for the sake of the future of worldwide kosen-rufu.

The new era of a youthful SGI is now underway.

Let us continue eternally to foster capable people, win with capable people, and open the way to peace and happiness with capable people.

I hope you will take leading roles in every sphere. Please build towering bastions of capable people wherever you carry out your mission.

32

BLAZE NEW TRAILS WHERE NONE HAVE EXISTED BEFORE

Those who strive for kosen-rufu are worthy of the highest respect. It doesn't matter what organizational positions they may have. We must always remember that those working and struggling the hardest in the most trying circumstances are the most noble.

Both the writings of Nichiren Daishonin and the Lotus Sutra are filled with praise for such individuals. Leaders need to cherish those who are challenging themselves and treat them with supreme respect. Faith shines in such sincere behavior.

It is not educational background or official titles that matter. As long as leaders have strong faith, the organization for kosen-rufu is certain to flourish. Their earnest efforts will inspire others to strive alongside them.

• • •

The personal growth of leaders fuels the development of the

organization. As leaders, therefore, I hope you will be people of action and initiative.

Joy lies in taking action. Human revolution lies in challenging oneself for kosen-rufu.

I hope you will strive actively in your practice of gongyo and chanting Nam-myoho-renge-kyo, tackling each problem before you, and work on transforming your lives for the better, one step at a time.

Bearing in mind the Daishonin's message to "strengthen your faith day by day and month after month" (WND-1, 997), please energetically blaze new trails where none have existed before.

* * *

Nothing is nobler than trying to come up with ways to actualize and expand kosen-rufu in our communities. Without such practical efforts, kosen-rufu is just an empty abstraction, a mere ideal.

Ultimately, the most important thing is to chant Nam-myoho-renge-kyo and bring forth your creativity and wisdom in your actual efforts for kosen-rufu. Please take personal responsibility, unite together with your fellow members, and forge on with firm determination.

Decide to win in the place where you are, chant, rack your brains, and struggle to make kosen-rufu advance in your community. That's the mark of a real champion. The heavenly deities will not fail to protect such a person.

Youth around the world are advancing vibrantly. A

wonderful new era has begun. I call on you, my friends in the youth division, to illuminate your communities and society as a whole with your optimism and positivity.

33

SGI MEETINGS ARE FOR STRENGTHENING OUR FAITH

SGI meetings are equivalent to the assembly where the Lotus Sutra was preached. They are infinitely noble realms of "many in body, one in mind," where kosen-rufu is carried out.

In "Expedient Means," the Lotus Sutra's second chapter, which we recite every morning and evening in gongyo, it states: "[The Thus Come Ones'] words are soft and gentle and can delight the hearts of the assembly" (LSOC, 57).

It's essential that leaders welcome everyone to meetings with the greatest sincerity, express heartfelt appreciation for their efforts, impart joy and peace of mind, and enable everyone to feel relaxed and refreshed. Strive to hold inspiring meetings that leave all the participants filled with courage and hope.

The way to achieve this is through chanting Nam-myoho-renge-kyo. Chant in preparation so that you are charged with life force when you attend the meeting. Revitalized in this way, please greet everyone brightly.

• • •

It is important that meetings be fresh and invigorating. They should revitalize everyone attending, spurring them to challenge themselves anew.

With the resolve to foster successors for the eternal perpetuation of the Law and to set in motion a new momentum for kosen-rufu, please chant Nam-myoho-renge-kyo, hold planning sessions with your fellow members, and come up with original and creative ideas for your meetings. Brimming with the Soka Gakkai spirit and striving with joy, wisdom, and common sense, please find ways to help everyone move in the direction of victory.

If you hold meetings where everyone feels glad to have attended and goes home with a refreshed determination, the vigor and energy of kosen-rufu will increase.

Please make sure that meetings end on time and are conducted safely. With each meeting, let's unite anew and advance afresh.

• • •

Nichiren Daishonin writes, "I want people with seeking minds to meet and read this letter together for encouragement" (WND-1, 306) Today, in accord with these words, people gather at our SGI meetings to study and encourage one another based on Nichiren's writings. They join together to polish and develop their lives; there are no other gatherings like them anywhere else.

Since my youth, when speaking at Soka Gakkai meetings or talking to people one on one about faith, I have always quoted and discussed passages from Nichiren's writings. Studying and practicing the world's foremost life philosophy with our peers is a source of unsurpassed joy.

I hope you will open the writings together with your fellow youth and discover a way forward to unassailable victory.

34

SET OUT ON A NEW YOUTHFUL JOURNEY

The SGI is an organization directly connected to Nichiren Daishonin, dedicated to realizing the vow for kosen-rufu in accord with the Buddha's intent and decree.

As we chant Nam-myoho-renge-kyo for ourselves and others, the same life state as the Daishonin wells forth powerfully within us.

It is just as Nichikan Shonin declares, "Through the power of the Mystic Law, we manifest the life of the Daishonin within ourselves."

In other words, we are all direct disciples of Nichiren Daishonin. We embrace the supreme Law for realizing happiness for ourselves and others. We all, without exception, have a noble mission.

Please be proud and confident that you are, indeed, the foremost youth in the world.

• • •

The Mystic Law is the fundamental source of revitalization. Our lives are based on the Mystic Law, which means that each day is time without beginning,* each day is a new challenge. I hope you will spend each day of your youth creating value and steadily continuing to grow and advance.

My mentor, Mr. Toda, said: "Should you feel as though you're stuck, bring forth the great power of faith, challenge your own weaknesses, triumph over them, and expand your state of life. This is the ongoing challenge of 'discarding the transient and revealing the true' in one's own life."

Never be discouraged, even if you don't see immediate results or things don't seem to be going as you had planned. Set forth anew each day, with perseverance and optimism. That is the way to genuine hope and fulfillment.

• • •

Mr. Toda taught me everything. I lived my youth with the determination to actualize all of his cherished goals for kosen-rufu and to steadfastly protect the precious organization he entrusted to me and ensure its further development.

I would like all of you, my young friends, to become outstanding individuals. Cheerfully encourage one another as you advance together as comrades who share a vow from time without beginning. May you together usher in a golden new era.

* Time without beginning (Jpn *kuon-ganjo*): A reference to each person's original state of life as a Buddha.

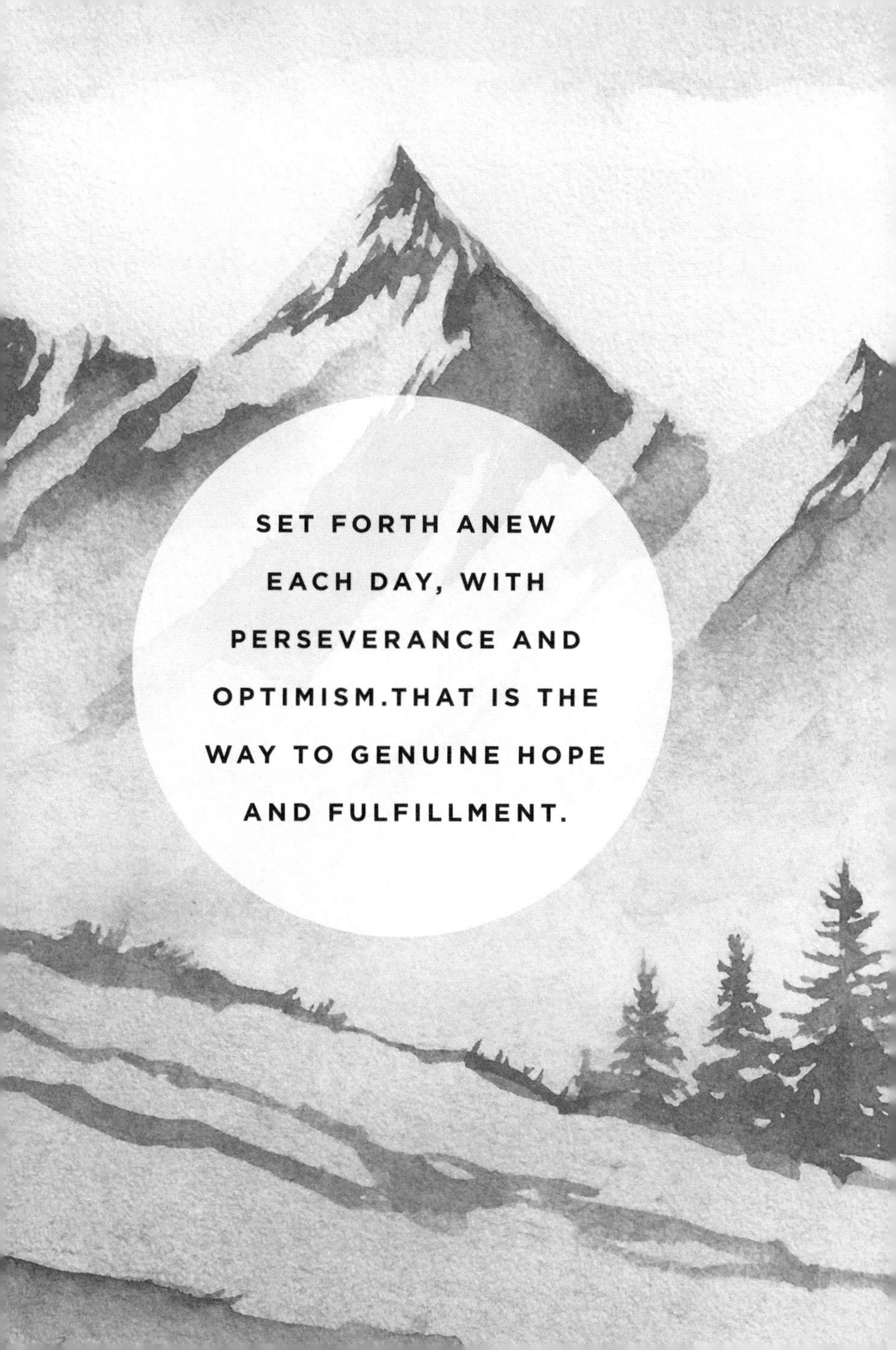

SET FORTH ANEW
EACH DAY, WITH
PERSEVERANCE AND
OPTIMISM.THAT IS THE
WAY TO GENUINE HOPE
AND FULFILLMENT.

35

EXPAND OUR NETWORK OF GOOD FRIENDS

Nothing is more important in leading a positive life than having good friends. That is because advancing with good friends is a source of growth and fulfillment.

The first step is to be a good friend to others. Be sincere and treasure each of your friends, and enjoy making new ones as well, creating a growing circle of friendship.

My mentor used to say, "Youth call forth other youth—that is how kosen-rufu will be realized!"

Please open your hearts, meet new people, and build a network of youth that will illuminate the future.

• • •

Make at least one really good friend with whom you can talk about anything. Find one good senior in faith to whom you can turn for advice and guidance when something happens. Having good friends and good seniors in faith will enable you to direct your life toward peace and happiness.

Nichiren Daishonin cites the Lotus Sutra passage "Thrust aside evil friends and associate with good companions" (WND-1, 832).

Stay away from unscrupulous individuals and do not let them come near you. These are troubled times, so please do not let "bad friends," or negative influences, sway you or take advantage of you.

I hope you will cheerfully forge ahead on the path of continuous victory with good, trustworthy friends.

• • •

The year-end holiday season is the perfect opportunity to get together with old friends that we don't see so often. We can also stay in touch by sending greeting cards.

Our behavior as a person is first and foremost. Be the kind of person who is delightful to be around and makes a favorable impression on others. That will lead to lively dialogue, friendship, and helping others form ties to Nichiren Buddhism.

Chant to the Gohonzon to develop into a person who can get along with others and win their trust.

Based on chanting Nam-myoho-renge-kyo, deepen your friendships with others and continue making new friends who understand and support our movement.

Kosen-rufu is a struggle to expand positive connections with others.

I hope you, the members of the youth division, will always be wise, insightful, courageous, and bold, enacting a drama of friendship around the world.

YOUR COURAGE IN STRIVING TO MAKE A BREAKTHROUGH IS CERTAIN TO RESONATE IN THE HEARTS OF OTHERS AND ACTIVATE THE PROTECTIVE FUNCTIONS OF THE UNIVERSE.

36

DISCUSSION MEETINGS ARE THE KEY TO VICTORY

The new era of worldwide kosen-rufu has arrived.

Let's make a fresh start from our discussion meetings, which are a proud Soka Gakkai tradition.

The February Campaign of 1952 in Kamata Chapter was a struggle fought and won based on discussion meetings. And the driving force for that victory was the youth.

It's important to have a spirit to include everyone at discussion meetings. The more this spirit spreads, the greater momentum our movement will gain.

Let's chant earnestly and prepare thoroughly to ensure the success of every meeting. Especially as leaders, it's important that we actively reach out to members and encourage them to attend. When the meeting is over, we should also thank them for attending and warmly see them off.

And let's always remember to sincerely thank and show utmost courtesy to the families who offer their homes as meeting places.

• • •

Sincere actions are a source of victory in all things. At meetings, therefore, please warmly greet each person with a spirit of care and respect.

There is no need to be discouraged if only a few people attend. In fact, small meetings where everyone can see one another are opportunities to talk heart to heart and really get to know one another.

The Lotus Sutra says that someone who teaches even a single phrase of the sutra to another is an envoy of the Buddha and is carrying out the Buddha's work (see LSOC, 200).

I would now like to call on the youth to carry on the unflagging Soka Gakkai spirit of our pioneering members—that of continuing to encourage and support each member, determined to help them stand up in faith.

• • •

In the midst of his life-threatening exile on Sado Island, Nichiren Daishonin solemnly declared, "Here I will make a great vow" (WND-1, 280).

As youth of the SGI, make a great vow and resolve to create an unprecedented record of achievement for kosen-rufu in your country and in the world.

We grow by breaking through our limitations. Difficult challenges deepen our prayers. Your courage in striving to make a breakthrough is certain to resonate in the hearts of others and activate the protective functions of the universe.

Please be assured that the efforts you are making now will pave the way toward the realization of worldwide kosen-rufu.

Chant, take action, and win each day with utmost confidence and pride.

I hope you will create a new record of achievement, adding another glorious page to the history of your youth.

37

LET'S INITIATE A NEW "MEETING REVOLUTION"

The atmosphere of a meeting is determined by the emcee's voice. A vibrant, refreshing voice will inspire those gathered and set a bright and positive mood.

SGI meetings could be likened to the assembly of the Lotus Sutra. Please prepare for meetings by sincerely chanting for everyone who attends to be able to embark vigorously on fresh victories in the spirit of "many in body, one in mind."

Your firm determination to hold a successful meeting will definitely bear fruit. As a youth, I, too, served as the emcee at numerous important events, including the Otaru Debate and the grand youth gathering with President Toda on March 16, 1958.

Nothing is more powerful than the voices of young people who live true to their convictions. Please rouse in everyone a spirit of joyful advance!

• • •

Nichiren Daishonin writes, "Those resolved to seek the way should gather [together]" (WND-1, 206). Gathering together with others is energizing. The engine for moving forward in our lives is turned on and the rhythm of our lives becomes more vibrant.

Please avoid one-sided communication, and instead create an environment that makes it easy for people to ask questions, clarify points they don't understand, or seek guidance.

Whenever someone asked Mr. Toda the kind of question that everyone wanted to ask or that provided the opportunity to talk about the deep principles of Buddhism, he would praise the questioner, saying: "That's an excellent question! Thank you!"

When discussions are filled with seeking spirit, members gain understanding and confidence. That understanding invigorates members' faith and allows them to take on new challenges.

• • •

Soka means "creating value." So let's hold meetings in a way that creates the greatest value. As leaders, please summon your wisdom and creativity to make meetings truly meaningful and worthwhile so that everyone is inspired to take action for kosen-rufu.

Our members all have different kinds of jobs and schedules, which may make it difficult for everyone to get together. Leaders mustn't exhaust members by insisting that they all gather together at some set time and place.

As leaders, your role is to support your fellow members and help guide them to happiness. Please continue to make efforts to visit each member individually. Home visits and personal guidance are the basis of SGI activities. I hope you will also take the lead in sharing Nichiren Buddhism with others.

Let's energetically go out to meet and support our friends again today!

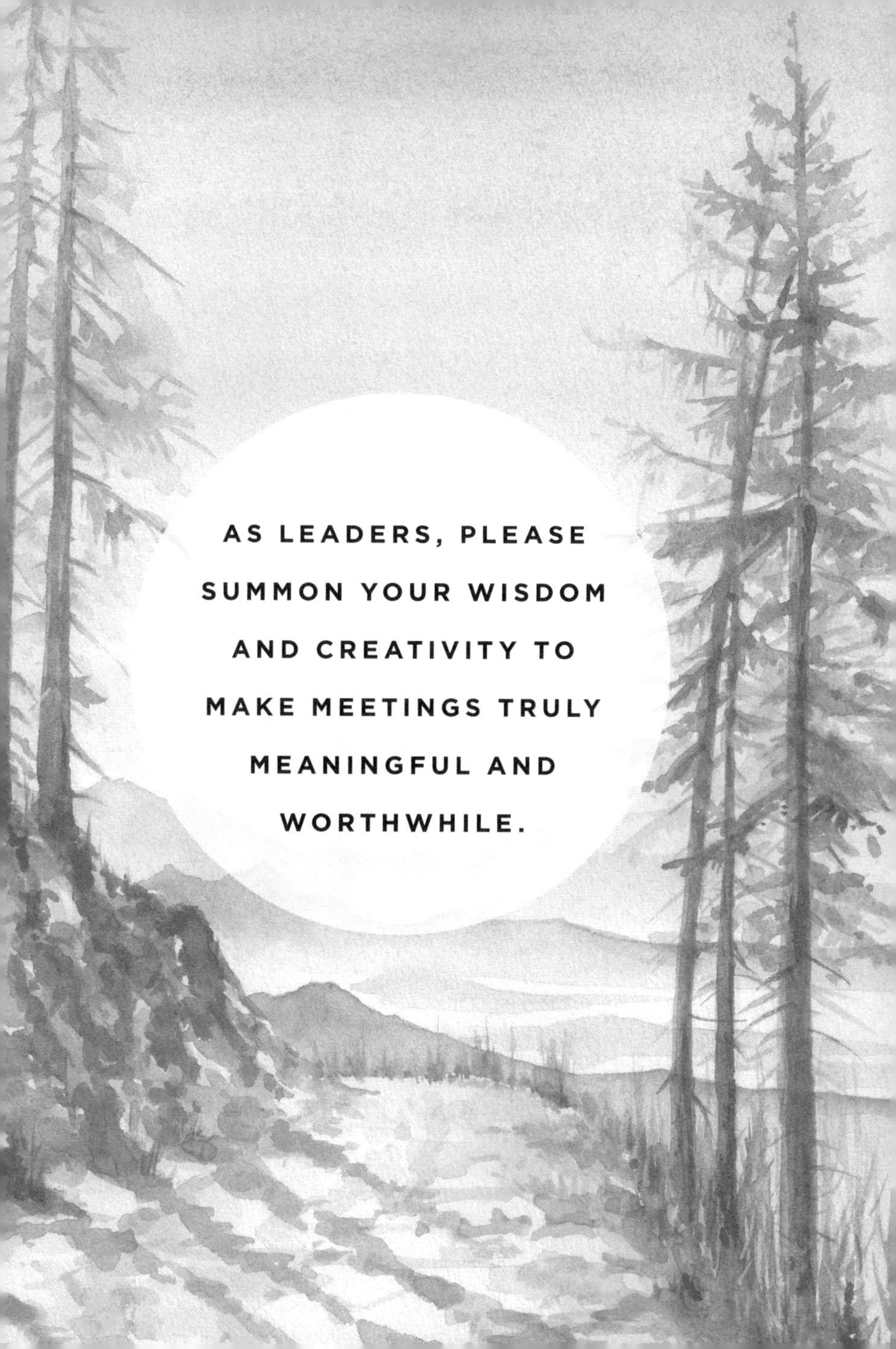

AS LEADERS, PLEASE SUMMON YOUR WISDOM AND CREATIVITY TO MAKE MEETINGS TRULY MEANINGFUL AND WORTHWHILE.

GLOSSARY

bodhisattva

One who aspires to enlightenment, or Buddhahood, and carries out altruistic practices. It also indicates a state of life characterized by compassion. The bodhisattva ideal is central to the Mahayana Buddhist tradition as the individual who seeks happiness both for him- or herself and for others.

Bodhisattvas of the Earth

An innumerable host of bodhisattvas who emerge from beneath the earth as described in "Emerging from the Earth," the fifteenth chapter of the Lotus Sutra. The Buddha, Shakyamuni, entrusts to them the task of propagation of the essence of the Lotus Sutra in the time after his death. Nichiren regarded those who embrace and propagate the teaching of the Mystic Law as Bodhisattvas of the Earth.

Buddha

Literally "Awakened One"; one who perceives the true nature of all life and who leads others to attain the same enlightenment. The Buddha nature or condition of Buddhahood exists within all beings and is characterized by the qualities of wisdom, courage, compassion, and life force. Historically this indicates Shakyamuni, the founder of Buddhism.

Buddhahood

The state of awakening a Buddha has attained. The ultimate goal of Buddhist practice and the highest of the Ten Worlds. The word *enlightenment* is often used synonymously with Buddhahood. Buddhahood is regarded as a state of perfect freedom, in which one is awakened to the eternal and ultimate truth that is the reality of all things. This supreme state of life is characterized by boundless wisdom and infinite compassion. The Lotus Sutra reveals that Buddhahood is a potential in the lives of all beings.

changing poison into medicine

The principle that earthly desires and suffering can be transformed into benefit and enlightenment by virtue of the power of the Law.

earthly desires are enlightenment

A Mahayana principle based on the view that one can attain enlightenment without eliminating earthly desires: they are one with and inseparable from enlightenment. While we cannot rid ourselves of earthly desires, we can use them as fuel to attain enlightenment when we chant Nam-myoho-renge-kyo.

establishing the correct teaching for the peace of the land

A principle of Nichiren Buddhism that explains that a people's fundamental beliefs are key in the realization of a peaceful society.

February Campaign
In February 1952, President Ikeda, then an adviser to Tokyo's Kamata Chapter, initiated a dynamic propagation campaign. Together with the Kamata members, he broke through the previous monthly record of some 100 new households by introducing Nichiren Buddhism to 201 new households.

Gohonzon
The scroll that serves as the object of devotion in Nichiren Buddhism. The Gohonzon embodies the eternal Law of the universe, Nam-myoho-renge-kyo, and the life condition of Buddhahood. SGI members chant to a Gohonzon enshrined in their own homes in order to bring forth the life state of Buddhahood from within.

gongyo
Literally, to "exert [oneself in] practice." This refers to the twice daily Nichiren Buddhist practice of reciting portions of the second and sixteenth chapters of the Lotus Sutra and chanting Nam-myoho-renge-kyo to the Gohonzon.

Hei no Saemon (d. 1293)
A leading official in the Hojo regency, the de facto ruling body of Japan during the Kamakura period. He wielded tremendous influence and collaborated with leading priests of established Buddhist schools of the day to persecute Nichiren and his followers.

human revolution

The term used by Josei Toda to describe a fundamental process of inner transformation whereby individuals can unleash the full potential of their lives and take control over their own destiny.

kosen-rufu

A Japanese phrase literally meaning "to declare and spread widely." It refers to the process of securing lasting peace and happiness for all humankind by establishing the humanistic ideals of Nichiren Buddhism in society. Kosen-rufu is often used synonymously with world peace, and more broadly it could be understood as a vision of social peace brought about by the widespread acceptance of core values such as unfailing respect for the dignity of human life.

Land of Tranquil Light

Also, Land of Eternally Tranquil Light. The Buddha land, which is free from impermanence and impurity. In contrast to other sutras, the Lotus Sutra says that this Buddha land is not some paradise far removed from the saha world and explains that the nature of the land is determined by the minds of its inhabitants.

Latter Day of the Law

The last of the three periods following the death of Shakyamuni Buddha—the Former, Middle, and Latter Days of the Law. In the Latter Day, Shakyamuni's teachings fall into confusion and lose their power to lead people to enlightenment. From the perspective of the Lotus Sutra, the Latter Day of the Law is the time when the teaching it contains, namely Nam-myoho-renge-kyo, will be spread widely.

Lotus Sutra

Widely recognized as one of the most important and influential sutras, or sacred scriptures, of Mahayana Buddhism. In the sutra, Shakyamuni reveals that all people can attain enlightenment and that Buddhahood—a condition of absolute happiness, freedom from fear and from all illusions—is inherent in all life.

March 16, 1958

The day on which six thousand youth from throughout Japan assembled with second Soka Gakkai president Josei Toda, just weeks before his death. It was a solemn ceremony of mentor and disciple—of the passing of the baton of the great undertaking of kosen-rufu. Having accomplished his cherished goal of reaching a membership of 750,000 households, Mr. Toda entrusted his youthful disciples with the full responsibility for the future of our movement. March 16, or Kosen-rufu Day, has since been one of the most solemn and profound anniversaries within the Soka Gakkai.

Mystic Law

The ultimate law, principle, or truth of life and the universe in Nichiren's teachings; the Law of Nam-myoho-renge-kyo.

Nam-myoho-renge-kyo

An invocation established by Nichiren on April 28, 1253. The title of the Lotus Sutra in its Japanese translation is Myoho-renge-kyo. To Nichiren, Nam-myoho-renge-kyo was the expression, in words, of the Law of life that all Buddhist teachings seek to clarify. Practitioners of Nichiren Buddhism chant Nam-myoho-renge-kyo as their core Buddhist practice. This is sometimes described as chanting *daimoku*.

Nichiren (1222–82)

A Buddhist reformer who lived in thirteenth-century Japan, often referred to by the honorific title "Daishonin" or "great sage." His intensive study of the Buddhist sutras convinced him that the Lotus Sutra contained the essence of the Buddha's enlightenment and that it held the key to transforming people's suffering and enabling the peaceful flourishing of society. Nichiren established the invocation of Nam-myoho-renge-kyo in 1253. His claims invited an onslaught of often violent persecutions from the military government and the established Buddhist schools. Throughout, he refused to compromise his principles to appease those in authority.

the oneness of mentor and disciple

The concept that disciples can reach the same state of Buddhahood as their mentor by practicing the teachings of the latter. In Nichiren Buddhism, this is the direct way to enlightenment, that is, to believe in the Gohonzon and practice according to the Daishonin's teachings. In addition, "oneness" expresses that the relationship between teacher and student, between mentor and disciple, must be based on the recognition that both possess the same noble potential—the potential for Buddhahood—and strive together to accomplish the same vow.

Osaka Campaign
A months-long propagation effort in Kansai, Japan, led by a young Daisaku Ikeda, who had been dispatched by second Soka Gakkai president Josei Toda. The campaign culminated in May 1956, during which the Kansai members introduced 11,111 households to the practice of Nichiren Buddhism, an impossible feat.

Otaru Debate
A public debate between Soka Gakkai representatives and priests of Nichiren Shu (the Minobu school of Nichiren Buddhism), held at the Otaru Civic Hall in the city of Otaru, Hokkaido, on March 11, 1955. The debate was won by the Soka Gakkai side. The incident is described in detail in volume nine of *The Human Revolution*.

saha world
Our present world, which is filled with suffering. Often translated as the world of endurance. In Sanskrit, *saha* means the earth; it derives from a root meaning "to bear" or "to endure." In this context, the saha world indicates a world in which people must endure suffering. It is also defined as an

impure land, a land defiled by earthly desires and illusion, in contrast with a pure land.

substituting faith for wisdom

The principle that faith is the true cause for gaining supreme wisdom, and faith alone leads to enlightenment. In general, Buddhism describes supreme wisdom as the cause of enlightenment. According to the Lotus Sutra, however, even Shariputra, who among the Buddha's ten major disciples was revered as foremost in wisdom, could attain enlightenment only through faith, not through wisdom. In other words, while the Buddha awakened to the truth through wisdom, we can attain the same state of enlightenment through having faith in and practicing the correct teaching of the Buddha.

Tatsunokuchi Persecution

An unsuccessful attempt, plotted by Hei no Saemon and corrupt priests, to execute Nichiren at Tatsunokuchi on the western outskirts of Kamakura in Japan in September 1271. A month later, he was sent into exile on the desolate Sado Island.

Thus Come One

Shakyamuni Buddha. One of the ten honorable titles of a Buddha, meaning one who has come from the realm of truth. This title indicates that a Buddha embodies the fundamental truth of all phenomena and has grasped the law of causality spanning past, present, and future.

transform karma into mission
The view of karma that the sufferings we go through now serve a profound purpose in our lives. Our karma gives us the opportunity to do our human revolution, overcome our problems, and thus become great examples of the power of faith, which in turn allows us to fulfill our mission for kosen-rufu.